The Trouble with Christianity

A Psychological Perspective

The Trouble with Christianity

A Psychological Perspective

Richard Oxtoby

CHRISTIAN
ALTERNATIVE

Winchester, UK
Washington, USA

First published by Christian Alternative Books, 2016
Christian Alternative Books is an imprint of John Hunt Publishing Ltd.,
Laurel House, Station Approach,
Alresford, Hants, SO24 9JH, UK
office1@jhpbooks.net
www.johnhuntpublishing.com
www.christian-alternative.com

For distributor details and how to order please visit the 'Ordering' section on our website.

Text copyright: Richard Oxtoby 2015

ISBN: 978 1 78535 289 8
Library of Congress Control Number: 2015958954

A CIP catalogue record for this book is available from the British Library.

Design: Lee Nash

Printed in the USA by Edwards Brothers Malloy

We operate a distinctive and ethical publishing philosophy in all areas of our business, from our global network of authors to production and worldwide distribution.

CONTENTS

A Sleep of Prisoners

The human heart can go the lengths of God.
Dark and cold we may be, but this
Is no winter now. The frozen misery
Of centuries breaks, cracks, begins to move;
The thunder is the thunder of the floes,
The thaw, the flood, the upstart spring.
Thank God our time is now when wrong
Comes up to face us everywhere,
Never to leave us till we take
The longest stride of soul we ever took.
Affairs are now soul size.
The enterprise
Is exploration into God.
Where are you making for? It takes
So many thousand years to wake
But will you wake for pity's sake!
  – Christopher Fry[1]

Dedicated with deep affection and gratitude
To all those, of whatever religious orientation, or none,
Who, when it comes to a choice between being right and
being kind,
Choose kind.

Introduction

You cannot shelter theology from science, or science from theology.
There is no short-cut to truth.
– Alfred North Whitehead. *Religion in the Making*

In writing this book it has been my aim to keep things as short as possible, in the belief that the longer a book is, the fewer people will read it, and it is my earnest hope that this book will have a wide readership. I hope that it will make a significant contribution to getting rid of some of the psychopathologies which have encrusted Christianity in the 2000 years or so of its existence. The message I seek to convey is a very simple one, much simpler than most of the often dense and confusing speculations to be found in much Christian Theology. That being so, I have tried to constantly bear in mind the warning of the eighteenth-century cleric, the Reverend James Ray to the effect that, 'He who useth many words in explaining his subject doth, like the cuttlefish, for the most part hide himself in his own ink.' I hope that I have struck the right balance between brevity and supplying enough technical detail[2] for readers to evaluate for themselves the quality of the ideas I am putting across in this book.

Those ideas have been maturing within me for more than half a century now. I first encountered Christianity at an early age in a religious environment in which being washed in the blood of the lamb and the idea of 'God' as having given us the 'priceless gift' of having his 'dearly beloved son' tortured and killed so that he could forgive us for our sins played no part. When as a young teenager there was a change of resident minister in the Methodist Church where my father was organist, I became aware that there was another side to Christianity. I was puzzled by my first

1

encounters with the theory of the Atonement, regarded by so many Christians as the central defining concept of their religion. It seemed an odd and quite unreal idea that had nothing to do with my life or the lives of my family and other friends. The dogma remained mostly out of consciousness somewhere in the back of my mind for many years, but my work as a psychotherapist, often encountering the destructive effect religion had had on so many of my clients, gradually led me to look at the doctrine more closely.

Some of the first fruits of that examination are evident in my *The Two Faces of Christianity*[3] but recent events have fired me with a determination to reinforce the theme I developed in that earlier book, and to redouble my efforts to persuade my fellow Christians to abandon a concept of God which is not just pointless and unhelpful in humanity's search for greater happiness, but is psychopathologically blunting of the spiritual sensitivities of those who hold that belief, and indeed, although I am reluctant to use a word favoured by those whose religious ideas are very different from my own, blasphemous.

The idea that there exists an omnipotent being in charge of the universe who was not merely unable to prevent, but actually decreed the suffering and death of his 'dearly beloved son' is about the most destructive idea I can imagine. A recent TV news item which included an account by a female victim of one of the illegal human traffickers operating in the Mediterranean at the moment, of how she had to watch another woman being raped by one of the crew, and then thrown into the sea to drown, is one of the most shocking things I have ever encountered.[4] It led me to imagine a conversation between the person who did that, and a would-be converter of that man to the religion of compassionate love for all embedded in the teachings of that inspired Jewish religious genius, Jesus of Nazareth. What could the Christian proselytiser say if the man (s)he was trying to convert were to respond to any criticism of his behaviour with something along the lines of, 'You're making too much of this woman's suffering. We've all got to suffer from time to time. Wasn't it even decreed by your God that his son whom he loved so much had to suffer and die? Is what I did to this woman any worse than what God did to his son?'

I do not believe that any believer in the truth of the Dogma of the Atonement would have any acceptable answer to that. And if he or she were to have responded with the extraordinary statement of Pope John Paul II that, 'Suffering, particularly in the later years of life, is part of God's saving plan for humanity,' (s)he would surely have lost for ever any chance of transforming the cruel behaviour of that particularly brutal rapist. The callous disregard for, and denigration of human happiness that that Papal statement demonstrates, is a vivid example of the corrupting effect of the Doctrine of the Atonement on the spiritual sensitivities of those in high places within the Christian Church.

It is a striking fact, and one still not known to many Christians, that in a recently rediscovered manuscript of the early Christian Church called *The Didache: The Lord's Teaching Through the Twelve Apostles to the Nations*, a description of the Eucharist (or communion) is given which makes no mention of the supposed sacrificial nature of Jesus' death. The late Geza Vermes, Emeritus Professor of Jewish Studies at Oxford University and described by *The Times* newspaper as 'the world's leading Gospel scholar' says of this book that it is, 'one of the most significant literary treasures of primitive Christianity.'[5] It is a manual of moral instruction and church practice, containing many of the sayings of Jesus, which claims to have been authored by the twelve apostles. It is dated by scholars as having been originally written somewhere between 50 and 120 CE[6], and was lost for hundreds of years, being only re-discovered in 1875 in the Jerusalem Monastery of the Holy Sepulchre at Constantinople. Far from quoting the words of the 'institution of the Lord's Supper' recorded in Matthew (26:26-28), Mark (14:22-24), and Luke (22:19-20), Chapter 9 of the Didache starts off with the words, 'Now concerning the Eucharist, give thanks this way.' First, concerning the cup:

> We thank thee, our Father, for the holy vine of David Thy servant, which You madest known to us through Jesus Thy servant; to Thee be the glory for ever.

And concerning the broken bread:

> We thank Thee, our Father, for the life and knowledge which You madest known to us through Jesus Thy Servant; to Thee be the glory for ever. Even as this broken bread was scattered over the hills, and was gathered together and became one, so let Thy Church be gathered together from the ends of the earth into Thy kingdom; for Thine is the glory and the power through Jesus Christ for ever.

At no point is any mention made of Jesus' death, or of its supposed atoning significance, nor of any belief that in partaking of the Eucharistic meal, Christians are eating the body and drinking the blood of Jesus, either literally or metaphorically, nor of a loving God who condemned his son to suffer and die for the sins of mankind.

Significantly the 'words of institution of the Lord's Supper' in Luke 22:19-20 ('This is my body which is given for you' and 'This cup that is poured out for you is the new covenant in my blood') were not present in the earliest and most reliable manuscript sources of that gospel.

Even more significantly, those words which appear in later manuscript versions of Luke's gospel, but not in the earliest ones, are almost identical with those that Paul in I Corinthians 11:23-25 puts into Jesus' mouth. Paul's reporting of anything from the life of Jesus without modifying and distorting it is a very rare event. Drawing the conclusion that Luke 22:19-20 is an interpolation into the original manuscripts of that Gospel by the early Church is almost irresistible. Whatever the truth of that situation may be, it is quite clear that the doctrine of the Atonement was very far from universally accepted in the early Christian Church.

In many ways this book should be seen as a companion volume to my *The Two Faces of Christianity* in which several of the issues that arise in the present book are discussed in much fuller detail. This present book, however, examines the fundamentally important concept of 'God' in greater depth than I was able to do in its longer 'big brother'. In that book I elaborated on an idea which one of Freud's 'disciples', Eric Fromm, introduced in his thought-provoking slim volume *Psychoanalysis and Religion*.

Fromm points out that there are two fundamentally different types of religion: Humanistic Religion and Authoritarian Religion. Realising that Christianity is not in fact one religion at all, but rather two completely different types of religion, the one humanistic and the other authoritarian existing under the same verbal label 'Christianity', has been quite a Damascus Road type of experience for me. That idea underlies all the thinking that I develop in this book. In fact it will doubtless become clear to the reader as he or she makes their way through it that if one wanted the briefest and simplest answer to the question posed in its title, my answer would be that the trouble with Christianity is that it has within itself an authoritarian as well as its core humanistic side, and that everything about Christianity which sabotages its attempts to make the world a better place, to bring about the Kingdom of God on earth, lies in the thinking of the authoritarian religion which shares the name of Christianity with a humanistic religion which contains a vastly different set of ideas.

Thomas Jefferson, the third President of the United States (1801-1809), and the principal author of the American Declaration of Independence of 1776, described the set of ethical

principles urged upon us by Jesus which make up that humanistic religion as providing the 'most sublime and benevolent code
of morals which has ever been offered to man'. I shall argue in
this book, amongst other things, that the root cause of the
'trouble with Christianity' lies in the fact that the authoritarian
branch of the Christian religion espouses an indefensibly
primitive concept of God, as compared with the very different
and empowering concept to be found in the religion of its
humanistic branch, which latter, unlike the former, is firmly
grounded in the ethical teachings of Jesus.

I have found Fromm's concept of the differences between
humanistic and authoritarian religions to be powerfully illumi-
nating in respect of my thinking about the good and the bad in
Christianity. It has helped me to understand some of the
otherwise seemingly inexplicable contradictions within the
religion, and to do what I can to help Christianity to achieve its
so far largely unrealised potential to make the world a better
place for all. I hope that readers of this book will find Fromm's
idea similarly enlightening.

Chapter 1

The Meaning of Words

It is not the case that our apprehension of a general truth is dependent on its accurate verbal expression. You cannot rise above the adequacy of the terms you employ.
– Alfred North Whitehead. *Religion in the Making*

Words, whether written or spoken, have no meaning in themselves. Their meaning, (which is at least subtly different for everyone who uses them) resides in the intellectual abstractions which make up the concept to which we attach those verbal labels (of, for example, an 'apple', a 'person', 'love', 'compassion', or 'hatred').

These abstractions are made by our nervous systems, and are of two types: Primary Abstractions and Higher-Order Abstractions. Primary Abstractions result from the interactions between our sensory receptors and the world around us in which we 'live, and move, and have our being'. They in turn become the raw material for Higher-Order abstractions. The contents of thought are a mixture of Primary and Higher-Order abstractions. The way in which both these types of abstractions arise is described in some detail in the next chapter.

Letters and words are part of the physical world: they belong in the same category as all the other physical things we encounter every day. The intellectual abstractions which make up the concepts we have of things, and which form the basis of all our intellectual activity however humble it might be, belong in a different category. They are part of the realm of non-physical reality[7], which is in no way either superior or inferior to concrete physical reality, but must not be confused with it. Assuming that intellectual abstractions are physical realities is to commit what the profound mathematical philosopher A. N. Whitehead described as, 'The Fallacy of Misplaced Concreteness'.[8]

It seems more and more clear to me that this fallacy lies at the root of many of the problems which academic, and sometimes everyday conversations run into from time to time. Prominent among these, and of particular interest and concern to me at the present time are the questions of the Existence of God, the Nature of Time and Space, and the so-called 'Mind-Body Problem' – the conundrum posed by the attempt to reconcile the fact that mental state and bodily condition are clearly closely related to each other, with the question that if 'the body' is understood to be a purely physical entity and 'the mind' to be at least partially defined as a non-physical entity, how can they possibly interact with each other?[9] In this book, my primary focus will be on 'The Concept of God' – does such a 'being' have any objective, 'real world' physical existence. It is my contention that many, perhaps most, Christians make erroneous judgments in this matter and that this is the most fundamental 'trouble' with Christianity.

Some readers may find the next chapter quite heavy going, and that they are not particularly interested in the technicalities of how concepts are formed. I hope that those readers who feel this way will simply skip to the end of the chapter and carry on reading from the last two paragraphs of that chapter.

Chapter 2

How Concepts are Formed

It is characteristic of the learned mind to exalt words. Yet mothers can ponder many things in their hearts which their lips cannot express. ... We know more of the characters of those who are dear to us than we can express accurately in words.
– Alfred North Whitehead. *Religion in the Making*

According to the ancient Greek philosopher Aristotle (384 to 322 BCE), human beings have five senses – Vision, Hearing, Touch, Smell, and Taste. Since Aristotle's time many more senses have been identified, now believed to be about 20 in number.[10] Some of these bring to our awareness various aspects of the physical environment both outside and inside our bodies, others (such as the electroreceptors which respond to changes in the electric fields around us) provide information which various systems within our body use, but of which we have no conscious awareness. There is no reason to think that we now have a complete listing of all the sensory receptors in the human body.

The basic unit responsible for the transmission and processing of information in the nervous system is the neurone. Most of the neurones in our body do their work by responding to the stimulation they receive at one of their ends (where the cell body is located) by releasing neurotransmitter chemicals from the terminal buttons at their other end. These in turn stimulate any other neurones with which they are connected (by means of a synapse) to discharge their dose of stimulating chemicals, and so the chain goes on, with many side-shoots and sometimes doublings back on themselves. With any one neurone (and there are estimated to be about 86 billion of them within the average human brain) making up to several thousand synaptic connections with other neurones, it is perhaps hardly surprising that it has been estimated that there are probably more than 1000 trillion neuronal connections in the human brain. It is this huge network of inter-connectedness which makes possible the remarkable feats of which the human being is capable.

Sensory receptors

Some of the total collection of neurones are modified in such a way that it is not the arrival of neurotransmitter chemicals from another neurone that stimulates them to release their own dose of chemicals onto the next neurone in the chain, but rather the receipt of physical stimulation (within certain upper and lower limits) from some other source, for example, sound within certain pitches and degrees of loudness, and light within a certain range of wavelengths and degrees of brightness.

Bundles of these specially modified neurones form the sensory receptors which constitute the interface between the physical world and our experience and understanding of it. Activity in these receptors is the first fundamental step in the process of converting the events of nature into our intellectual knowledge about those events.

Four things are particularly important to know and remember about the performance of our sensory receptors. Most fundamentally, our nervous systems are inevitably digital processing systems which convert the processes of continuous change within the human body into a series of digital events. I describe the system as *inevitably* a digital one because every neurone, whether it is part of a sensory receptor or just involved in transmitting information, acts in an 'all or none' manner, not becoming active until it has received a certain minimum amount of stimulation which causes it to 'fire', and release a dose of its own neurotransmitter onto the next neurone in the chain of which it is a part. In this way it is acting as an analogue to digital converter, aggregating the total of all the events influencing it between each digital signal into a single digital event.

Each of those single digital events gives a useful summary of the total amount of stimulation received since the previous one, but gives no information about the moment by moment subtle changes continually taking place in the neurone's environment. It is of course possible that there are other components of the brain which provide such more detailed information, but if there are, we as yet know nothing about them. Certainly so far as what we do know about the nervous system's role in transmitting and processing information, some detail starts to be lost at the level of the most basic communication-units in the system.

The second very important characteristic of our sensory receptors is that each receptor responds only to *changes* in environmental stimulation: a constant unchanging stimulus eventually ceases to initiate any response from a receptor. Thirdly, each different type of receptor responds only to changes in certain types of stimulation. For example, light waves, so far as we know, do not cause any response from our taste or smell receptors. And finally each receptor responds only to changes in a particular type of stimulation within certain limits. For example, unless these occur within a certain range of frequencies, the organ of hearing within the ear does not respond to the changes in air pressure, the alternating waves of compaction and rarefaction of the molecules of air which, when they occur within a certain range of frequencies, give rise to the sensation of sound. Events whose physical characteristics fall below a certain point exert no influence on a receptor, while those that fall above it either produce no effect, or they damage or even destroy the receptor – for example, exposure to light which is too bright can lead to blindness, and to sound which is too loud, to deafness.

Because the unaided human body is not able to respond to stimulation which is outside certain limits, unchanging, and of certain types, (for example, we have no direct bodily means of detecting the presence of radioactive radiation) an important part of the work of scientists and engineers has been devoted to designing and constructing equipment which converts changes in things for which we have no natural receptors into forms of energy-change which we can become aware of – for example, the movement of a pointer on a dial or changes in a numerical digital display, or perhaps variations in the pitch of a sound. Although some impressive successes have been achieved in this field, there is no way of knowing what sort of energy changes may be going on in our internal and external environment of which we are completely unaware, and therefore for the detection of which no equipment has yet been developed. As the eminent twentieth-century British Biologist J. B. S. Haldane asserted, 'The world is not only stranger than we suppose, it is stranger than we can suppose,' a profound truth which not just scientists, but anyone making any pronouncements about the 'nature of reality' needs to constantly remember.

The limitations of all intellectual knowledge

It follows from the above that all our intellectual knowledge is of necessity only a partial picture of what that knowledge is about. There is more to any particular 'violin', or 'chair', or 'toenail', or any other aspect of the universe than we can ever capture in words. This fact has enormous implications for all discussions about religion, spirituality, love, and indeed any and every aspect of life in general.

So far I have discussed only the way in which our sensory receptors extract a limited amount of information, albeit highly focussed information, from the environment in which we exist. These abstractions are the raw material out of which all our perceptions are constructed. But this abstracting property of our nervous systems is not restricted to the domain of sensorily-derived input. The whole structure of neurones is hierarchically-organised in such a way that large quantities of information are reduced to a more limited number of what we experience as abstract principles at progressively higher and higher levels of abstraction. If we call the abstractions derived from the activity of our sensory receptors Level 1 abstractions, the continuously present abstractive process (constantly active as long as our nervous systems are functioning) operates on those abstractions themselves to form what we might call Level 2 abstractions. These in turn become the basis of Level 3 abstractions, and so the process continues for as long as we are thinking. The concepts to which we attach words like 'water', 'soil', 'bread' and 'dog' are relatively low-level abstractions. The concepts to which we attach verbal labels such as 'imagination', 'peace', 'happiness', and 'misery' are much higher-level abstractions: the final abstractive process is just the last of a long series of abstractive processes that have preceded it.

This process of the generation of a set of abstractions of ever-higher degrees of generality is what underlies all thought. It is because the physiological process of abstraction exists that we are able to sometimes see that a number of similar things and events are instances of a single general principle. If we were unable to see any general principles operating in the world we would have to use every bit of our brain power to process the millions of separate bits of information that our sensory receptors deliver to us every day. Our minds would be choked with a surfeit of information, and the concept of knowledge would be meaningless. In A. N. Whitehead's vivid phrase, the process of abstraction is the way in which 'the infinitude of irrelevance is kept out of thought'.

The basic building blocks of the language in which we express our thoughts are the verbal labels we attach to the abstractions which are usually generated automatically, and totally unconsciously, by our nervous systems.

Our language thus consists of words whose meaning resides in the chain of abstractions to which those words have, by agreed convention among the users of the language, been consistently attached. The important thing to remember in any discussion about the nature of reality is that some words are linked to aspects of the physical world through fairly short chains of abstractions, words like 'flower' and 'tortoise' for example. Others like 'fantasy' and 'forgiveness' are linked to aspects of the physical world through relatively long, and sometimes very long chains of abstractions.

What this means is that the fact that we have a name for something does not mean that the thing so named has any real **physical** existence. The whole argument between atheists and those who assert that God exists is actually about whether or not the word 'God' refers directly to something which exists in the physical world, or whether or not it refers to something which exists only as an abstraction in the thought processes of human beings. If the latter, is the set of abstractions so labelled drawn from real-life human experiences, or from fantasies created by, for example, the very human desire for feelings of safety and security – to feel that there is a powerful someone or something looking after us (provided of course, that we behave ourselves!)?

In this book I shall argue that insofar as within Christianity the term God, (the central and most fundamental concept within any religion) is regarded as referring to a property of the universe of the same general type as the Force of Gravity, the Strong and Weak Nuclear Forces and the Electrostatic Force, then there is nothing irrational in its fundamental concept. More than that, if that property refers to certain established psychological facts about the effects of various forms of behaviour on human experience, then Christianity has a chance of being a potentially hugely powerful force for good in the world. It could inspire even more widespread efforts than it has so far, to make the world a better place – to increase the sum total of human happiness and to decrease the amount of pain, suffering and misery which at present abounds so horrifyingly in the world.

On the other hand, insofar as Christianity continues to retain at its heart the concept of God as a 'being' who is some sort of invisible Superman, Super Scientist, Super Engineer and/or Super Policeman, an old man, with or without a beard, who lives somewhere 'above the deep blue sky', with the further properties encapsulated in its Atonement Dogma, of an omnipotent God who is a cruel, controlling despot who created the universe, and despite being all-powerful, had, contradic-torily enough, no option but to create it containing flawed human beings who could only be saved the eternal punishment their wickedness demanded by sacrificing his 'dearly beloved son' to a horrible and painful death, Christianity will become more and more sidelined in the lives of ordinary human beings in their attempts to make the world a more humane place. As discussed at greater length in my *The Two Faces of Christianity*, the theory of the Atonement is so full of logical flaws, and so contra-dictory of the ethical principles of its appointed leader, Jesus Christ, as to invalidate any religion espousing it, for any role in perfecting human life and behaviour. Insofar as Christianity retains such a barbaric concept in its core, it will remain largely powerless to put an end to cruelty, war and other humanly-caused suffering.

Chapter 3

The Nature of God

To-day there is but one religious dogma in debate: What do you mean by 'God'? And in this respect, to-day is like all its yesterdays. This is the fundamental religious dogma, and all other dogmas are subsidiary to it.
– Alfred North Whitehead. *Religion in the Making*

The most fundamental thing wrong with Christianity, (and the religion as a whole is a very mixed bag of by no means fully consistent ideas), is that the concept of God held by many Christians is completely at variance with what is implied by Jesus' ethical principles. I believe that those aspects of the nature of language expounded so far in this book provide a rational basis for establishing a better concept of God than that which many people believe lies at the heart of Christianity.

The ethical principles of Jesus

What are the ethical principles which Jesus suggested we should apply in our dealings with the world? Briefly, they are that we are helping to create the Kingdom of Heaven (a place of perfect happiness) on earth when our behaviour is guided by a non-judgemental, compassionate love for all (and 'all' most importantly includes ourselves) which regards the welfare of people as more important than obedience to any moral injunctions just for their own sake. When we are inspired by this love, our behaviour is marked by authenticity (in which there is harmony between the values we claim to hold dear and the way we behave – the opposite of hypocrisy), meekness and humility when appropriate (rather than arrogance), the realisation that gentleness is ultimately stronger than violence, and the experience of finding that we often gain sometimes surprisingly pleasant benefits for ourselves when we do good to others. I briefly summarise below the much fuller discussion of these principles to be found in Chapter 5 of my *The Two Faces of Christianity*.

1. Compassionate love

The fundamental ethical imperative of Jesus' conception of the Kingdom of God is a humanistic one – to live a life filled with compassionate love for all. When asked by one of the Pharisees, 'Which commandment in the law is greatest?' he did not go to any of the Ten Commandments (such as 'Thou shalt not kill', and 'Thou shalt not commit adultery') or to any of the 'Thou shalt not' injunctions elsewhere in the Old Testament, but rather singled out the two commands to love to be found in Deuteronomy 6:5 and 11:13, and in Leviticus 19:18:

> Thou shalt love the Lord thy God with all they heart, and with all thy soul, and with all thy mind. This is the first and great commandment, and the second is like unto it, Thou shalt love thy neighbour as thyself (Matthew 22:37-40).[11]

As the German/American theologian Paul Tillich summarised it, for Jesus, 'Love is the ultimate law'. William Temple, the mid-twentieth-century Archbishop of Canterbury expressed the same thought when he wrote, 'There is only one ultimate and invariable duty, and its formula is, "Thou shalt love thy neighbour as thyself."' With realistic honesty he added, 'How to do this is another question, but this is the whole of moral duty.' As we all know all too well, that question of how to always show that love is a huge one.

One aspect of the answer to it is vividly illustrated in Jesus' parable of the Good Samaritan which is quoted in the gospels of Mathew, Mark, and Luke. In verses 30 to 35 of Chapter 10 of Luke's gospel we read:

And Jesus answering said, A certain man went down from Jerusalem to Jericho, and fell among thieves, which stripped him of his raiment, and wounded him, and departed, leaving him half dead. And by chance there came down a certain priest that way: and when he saw him he passed by on the other side. And likewise a Levite, when he was at the place, came and looked on him, and passed by on the other side. But a certain Samaritan, as he journeyed, came where he was: and when he saw him, he had compassion on him. And went to him and bound up his wounds, pouring in oil and wine, and set him on his own beast, and brought him to an inn, and took care of him. And on the morrow when he departed, he took out two pence, and gave them to the host, and said unto him, Take care of him, and whatsoever thou spendest more, when I come again I will repay thee.

The message Jesus was trying to put across in that parable was clearly a positive one towards the kind Samaritan, with a sub-text that social outcasts may well sometimes show greater virtuous behaviour than some pillars of the community. It is sad and deeply regrettable that those of us who regard ourselves as Christians, in other words as 'Followers of Christ', so often fail to manifest this Christian virtue in our dealings with not just wrongdoers and beggars in the street, but with ordinary human beings, and sometimes with our fellow religionists, and even with members of our own families.

In the biblical record, because of the limitations of the thought world at the time the gospels were written, it is just human beings who are mentioned as needing to be treated with compassionate love, but the influential twentieth-century humanitarian philosopher, theologian and medical missionary Albert Schweitzer, with his concept of Reverence for Life extended the reach of this all-important ethical attitude of compassionate love to more than just human beings. In his *Civilisation and Ethics*

Schweitzer argued that notwithstanding the inevitability of death for some living things in nature in order to support the continued life of others, all life has the right to exist and we have a fundamental ethical obligation to keep the amount of pain, death, and destruction in the universe to the absolute minimum. We should never arbitrarily terminate the life of any living thing just because we have the power, and feel the impulse, to do so.

Schweitzer writes movingly of the attitudes and behaviours towards the 'lower animals' of those imbued with the spirit of Reverence for Life.

A man is truly ethical only when he obeys the compulsion to help all life which he is able to assist, and shrinks from injuring anything that lives. ... If he walks on the road after a shower and sees an earthworm which has strayed onto it, he bethinks himself that it must get dried up in the sun if it does not return soon enough to ground into which it can burrow, so he lifts it from the deadly stone surface, and puts it on the grass. If he comes across an insect which has fallen into a puddle, he stops a moment in order to hold out a leaf or a stalk on which it can save itself.[12]

For Schweitzer, holding to the principle of Reverence for Life means preserving as far as possible the individual's pain-free health and happiness in a richly fulfilling life.

As in my own will-to-live there is a longing for wider life and for the mysterious exaltation of the will-to-live which we call pleasure, with dread of annihilation and of the mysterious depreciation of the will-to-live which we call pain; so it is also in the will-to-live all around me, whether it can express itself before me, or remains dumb.[13]

But for Schweitzer the principle of Reverence for Life extends even further – to keeping to an absolute minimum the destruction of beauty, man-made or in nature. Contemplating and preserving such beauty provides a powerful enhancement of the ability of all of us who have a deep Reverence for Life to enjoy our lives, and for those other creatures whose lives we so passionately seek to preserve to enjoy theirs. Schweitzer's reflections on this theme have a helpful relevance to Christian thinking about the inter-relationships between Goodness, Beauty, and Truth discussed in the next chapter.

As I say in my discussion of his thinking in Appendix 3 of *The Two Faces of Christianity*, Schweitzer who lived through two world wars was well aware of the strength of the societal forces individuals experience to suppress many aspects of their instinctual compassionate impulses. The operation of the psychological defence mechanism of Reaction Formation leads many people who are embarrassed by the stirrings of tender feelings within themselves to react with apparent scorn towards the behaviours and beliefs of those who feel deeply for the sufferings of others. Towards the end of his book, *Civilization and Ethics*, Schweitzer writes of those who embrace the principle of Reverence for Life:

He is not afraid of being laughed at as sentimental. It is the fate of every truth to be a subject for laughter until it is generally recognized. Once it was considered folly to assume that men of colour were really men and ought to be treated as such, but the folly has become an accepted truth. Today it is thought to be going too far to declare that constant regard for everything that lives, down to the lowest manifestations of life, is a demand made by rational ethics. The time is coming, however, when people will be astonished that mankind needed so long a time to learn to regard thoughtless injury to life as incompatible with ethics. Ethics are responsibility without limit towards all that lives.[14]

The rootedness of an attitude of Reverence for Life in the ethical principles espoused by Jesus which provide the bedrock on which Humanistic Christianity rests makes this topic highly relevant in any discussion of what abstractions are legitimately part of a Christian concept of God. Schweitzer's own assessment of the significance of what he has done in developing the concept of Reverence for Life is that:

> The ethic of Reverence for Life is the ethic of Jesus brought to philosophical expression, extended into cosmical form, and conceived of as ethically necessary.[15]

Compassionate love for all living creatures and the desire to make their lives as happy and deeply satisfying as possible is the fundamental characteristic which permeates the thinking of those who identify themselves as Humanistic Christians.

2. People before principles

Another of Albert Schweitzer's invaluable contributions to our thinking about the concept of God is his paraphrasing of Jesus' reported assertion that, 'The Sabbath was made for man, not man for the Sabbath' as, 'Never sacrifice a person to a principle'.

The sacrificing of the satisfaction of people's wishes, and sometimes of their needs to strict adherence to a set of rigid rules and regulations is typical of what happens in authoritarian organisations in general, and it certainly happens all too frequently where authoritarian Christianity is concerned. Obedience to 'God's will' (as authoritarian church leaders are wont to package their attempts to control the behaviour of adherents to their religion) is often seen as a central requirement for church members.

Humanistic Christianity requires a more flexible approach to discussion of what the rights and wrongs of various forms of human behaviour are. One of the more helpful attempts to provide this was made by Joseph Fletcher, a former Professor of Social Ethics at the Episcopal Theological School, Cambridge, Massachusetts with his concept of Situational Ethics.[16]

Situational Ethics has as its most basic principle (as it was for Jesus) that, 'There is only one thing that is always good and right, intrinsically good regardless of the context, and that one thing is love'. In the case of all other ethical and moral principles their 'rightness' depends on the consequences of applying them in any specific situation. Each ethical principle and moral commandment (for example, 'Thou shalt not kill') is neither good nor bad in itself. Its ethical soundness depends on the outcome for human welfare of its application in any particular situation. Fletcher quotes with approval A. N. Whitehead's dictum that, 'The simple-minded use of the notion 'right or wrong' is one of the chief obstacles to the progress of understanding'.[17]

Situational Ethics provides a framework for moral decision-making which is the antithesis of legalistic adherence to rigid moral principles which ignores Jesus' profound truth that the Sabbath, like all ethical and moral principles, exists only to make the world a better place for all. The realities of any particular situation, properly understood, may require disregard of one or more subsidiary ethical and moral principles, if the one inviolable overarching principle of, 'There is only one thing that is always good and right, intrinsically good regardless of the context, and that one thing is love' is not to be contravened. The application of any moral principle to any specific case which does not lead to an increase in human happiness is not bringing the Kingdom of God closer to us, no matter how valuable that principle may in general be.

Two quotes from Joseph Fletcher's book illustrate particularly powerfully the general principle he has formulated there. The first relates to a play, *The Rainmaker*, written by Richard Nash and all too little known today. In the 1950s when it was first performed in New York it made a considerable impact, was translated into more than 40 languages, and was made into both a film and a Broadway musical.

> The key to (the play) ethically, lies in a scene where the morally outraged brother of a lonely, spinsterized girl threatens to shoot the sympathetic but not 'serious' Rainmaker because he makes love to her in the barn at midnight. The Rainmaker's intention is to restore her sense of womanliness and her hopes for marriage and children. Her father, a wise old rancher, grabs the pistol away from his son, saying, 'Noah, you're so full of what's right, you can't see what's good.'[18]

The second quote makes the same point, but even more powerfully.

> The Christian Situation Ethicist agrees with Bertrand Russell and his implied judgment, 'To this day Christians think an adulterer more wicked than a politician who takes bribes, although the latter probably does a thousand times as much harm,' and he thoroughly rejects Cardinal Newman's view: 'The Church holds that it were better for sun and moon to drop from heaven, for the earth to fail, and for all the many millions who are upon it to die of starvation in extremist agony than ... that one soul, I will not say should be lost, but should commit one single venial sin.'[19]

The idea of God as a coercive force trying to impose 'his will' on humanity, however good that will might be, has no place in the concept of God as conceived by the Humanistic Christian.

3. Non-judgementalness
Closely related to the idea of making ethical principles subordinate to questions of human well-being is an attitude of caution to the making of moral judgements. Of course we all do, and

necessarily must sometimes form an opinion as to whether someone else's (or our own) behaviour is right or wrong. It is not the making of moral judgements which from a Humanistic Christian perspective is wrong, but rather the way some people communicate any negative judgement they have come to. What little we know of Jesus' teaching indicates that he believed it was more helpful to adopt a forgiving and understanding approach to wrongdoing, aimed at improving future behaviour, than to behave punitively towards the offender. To the extent that people realise their own shortcomings, and are quick to feel that, 'There but for the grace of God go I', angry expressions of moral outrage will not be part of their repertoire of behaviours. The way in which Jesus' 'Let he that is without sin cast the first stone' pricked the bubble of self-righteous condemnatory anger of the crowd baying for the blood of the woman who had been 'taken in adultery' (reported in John 8:7), is a masterly lesson in how judgemental anger can be defused.

The arrogance and self-deception involved in holier-than-thou moralising was obviously something that jarred very strongly with Jesus' attitude to 'sin'. Verses 9 to 14 of Chapter 18 of Luke's gospel, records a parable Jesus told his listeners which contrasted the unacceptable behaviour of a Pharisee who prayed publicly in the temple, thanking God that he was not a sinner 'like other people are' and praising his own impeccable religious credentials, with that of a nearby tax collector who was beating his breast and saying, 'God, be merciful to me, a sinner'. Jesus ends the parable in verse 14, with the words, '... for all who exalt themselves will be humbled, but all who humble themselves will be exalted'.

A large part of Chapter 23 of Matthew's gospel is devoted to a scathing attack on the behaviour of the scribes and Pharisees. Seven of these verses (13, 14, 15, 16, 23, 25, and 27) start with the emotional-tension-building words 'Woe unto you', while all but verse 16 have the addition of the words 'scribes and Pharisees, hypocrites' to the initial warning of woe to come.

The repetition of those words 'Woe unto you, scribes and Pharisees, hypocrites', followed in each case by a description of an instance of the sort of hypocrisy which particularly aroused Jesus' anger, creates an almost menacingly hypnotic effect. Whether Jesus ever expressed himself in exactly the way the gospel records suggest that he did, is doubtful. Those scriptures certainly do not contain a verbatim record of exactly what Jesus said on any subject, and the record we have of what he did say is more a record of what the gospel writers understood of Jesus' meaning than of what he actually said.

Nevertheless, although there were doubtless elements in the early Christian Church who took delight in vilifying Jewish religion and those who belonged to it, it seems likely that 'the woes' as they are called, do reflect something of how Jesus felt about those who did not practise what they preached. Unfortunately for Christian self-aggrandisement, hypocrisy in religious matters was never just confined to some individuals in Jewish religion – it has occurred, and still does occur frequently within Christianity.

There is, however, an additional reason for we human beings to be wary about pronouncing moral judgements, and that is that whenever we do so, we put on display for public evaluation the values that we have in terms of which we make those judgements. Some people will approve of those values and others will not, but Jesus' 'Judge not that ye be not judged' guideline is a friendly warning about the danger we put ourselves in when we make our moral judgements public, the danger of being perhaps thought poorly of for having the standards of judgement we have.

The humility and awareness of our own faults which Jesus obviously valued highly and urged upon us in respect of passing judgment on others, is just one of a number of ways in which behaviour consistent with being 'in the Kingdom of God' differs from that of those who use arrogant putdowns of those they fear might outshine them in their attempts to become highly regarded in the eyes of the world.

4. Mutuality/reciprocity

A central feature of Jesus' beliefs about the ethics of the Kingdom of God is the claim that, far from doing good to others necessarily involving sacrificing the satisfaction of our own needs (although sometimes we might cheerfully do that), most of the time in doing good to others we are receiving a benefit to ourselves as well, not least in terms of feeling good about what a kind, generous, and helpful person we are. The nineteenth-century American Unitarian philosopher and essayist Ralph Waldo Emerson, expressed a great psychological as well as spiritual truth when he said, 'It is one of the most beautiful compensations of this life that no man can sincerely try to help another without helping himself. ... Serve and thus you shall be served.'

This insight into the reciprocal benefits that accrue to both parties in compassionately loving interactions is an echo of the end of that beautiful prayer attributed to St Francis of Assisi, 'It is in giving that we receive; It is in forgiving others that we ourselves are forgiven.' For the Humanistic Christian, this aspect of 'the way the universe is' is a fundamentally important component of that bundle of intellectual abstractions to which the word God is most appropriately attached.

5. Inversion of the power hierarchy which commonly exists in those parts of the world untouched by deeply spiritual values.

One of the particularly distinctive features of the ethics of Jesus is his view that in the Kingdom of Heaven traditional 'worldly values' as to what constitutes success in life, and how to achieve it are stood on their head. For Jesus, the Kingdom of heaven is not a place where success in life[20] results from the aggressive pursuit of naked power, in which WIN-LOSE outcomes are sought whenever conflict is encountered.

For Jesus, gentleness is ultimately stronger than violence, and the greater desirability of meekness and humility than an attitude of arrogant superiority towards ourselves over other people, is well illustrated by the high regard he obviously had for the simplicity of the mind of a child. In that simplicity, before the harsh realities of many people's lives turned them to a greater or lesser extent, into hard-bitten, confirmed cynics, Jesus doubtless instinctively saw the manifestation of that oneness with spiritual things from which compassionate love springs. For those in whom the development of psychological defence mechanisms has not been so thoroughgoing as to cause them to close their minds to such issues, the sense of a loss of spiritual sensitivity with increasing age and life experience is often palpable.

That feeling of loss is probably at the root of all nostalgic longing for the return of some emotional experiences of the past. Perhaps some awareness of this is what led the band A-ha, when they wrote the song, *Forever not yours*, to include the lines, "Memories keep coming through, the good ones hurt more than the bad ones do." Thomas Hood, the early nineteenth-century English poet in his poem about childhood, *I remember, I remember*, captures this feeling well, and echoes the sentiments of Jesus when he said, as reported in verse 14 of Chapter 19 of Matthew's gospel, 'Let the little children come to me, and do not stop them; for it is to such as these that the kingdom of heaven belongs.'

I remember, I remember,
The house where I was born,
The little window where the sun
Came peeping in at morn;
He never came a wink too soon,
Nor brought too long a day,
But now, I often wish the night
Had borne my breath away.

I remember, I remember,
The roses, red and white;
The violets and the lily-cups,
Those flowers made of light!
The lilacs where the robin built,
And where my brother set
The laburnum on his birthday –
The tree is living yet!

I remember, I remember,
Where I used to swing;
And thought the air must rush as fresh
To swallows on the wing:
My spirit flew in feathers then,
That is so heavy now,
And summer pools could hardly cool
The fever on my brow!

I remember, I remember,
The fir trees dark and high;
I used to think their slender tops
Were close against the sky:
It was a childish ignorance,
But now 'tis little joy
To know I'm farther off from heav'n
Than when I was a boy."

6. Authenticity

One thing that Jesus seems to have felt particularly strongly about, so far as we can tell from the record of his life and teachings in the New Testament Gospel accounts, is hypocrisy, not being authentic in one's presentation of oneself to the world. As examined in the section on non-judgementalness above, Jesus is reported to have had harsh words for the scribes and Pharisees who in verses 27 and 28 of Chapter 23 of Matthew's gospel he describes as:

> … like unto whited sepulchers, which indeed appear beautiful outward, but are within full of dead men's bones, and of all uncleanness. Even so ye outwardly appear righteous unto men, but within ye are full of hypocrisy and iniquity.

Not many Christian thought leaders have given much attention to this question, and the whole tone of much conventional Christianity with its emphasis on the terrible consequences which will befall us if we do not always 'do the right thing' has militated against much honesty among Christians about any doubts they might have about the correctness of the beliefs they feel they are supposed to espouse as Christians.

One prominent churchman who was outspoken in his support for the importance Jesus attached to authenticity, was the thirteenth-century Roman Catholic saint, Thomas Aquinas. *Chambers Biographical Dictionary*[21] describes him as having 'exercised enormous intellectual authority throughout the Church'. That is doubtless true, but for all that, Aquinas's belief that a necessary property of all truly moral behaviour is being true to one's own conscience (sense of integrity), even in matters which the Church would call mortal sin, seems to have had relatively little impact on the attitudes of that institution.[22] Three centuries later another Roman Catholic saint, Ignatius Loyola, who founded the Society of Jesus, the Jesuits, expressed a view absolutely contradictory of Aquinas's. In his book *Rules For Thinking Within The Church*, he wrote, 'If the church should have defined anything to be black which to our eyes appears white, we ought in like manner to pronounce it black.'

Requiring any inauthentic expression of unconditional assent to any rigid dogma is an outright contradiction of what Jesus clearly believed was appropriate behaviour for those who sought to establish the Kingdom of Heaven in the kingdoms of this earth.

The nature of God

At the heart of each belief in the set of principles above is an abstraction. Bundled together these form a consistent and meaningful concept to which the Humanistic Christian feels it is appropriate to apply the verbal label 'God'. Defined in this way, 'God' is a property of the universe, a way of describing how things work in their spiritual/emotional/psychological aspect. On this view, God is an entity, a 'thing' of the same general type as the Force of Gravity and all the other fundamental forces of nature that have been studied by scientists. These forces are not physical entities which operate from outside the universe to make things happen within that universe, and neither is God an entity outside the universe who operates on it to make things happen (or not happen!) within it. The Force of Gravity is just a description of the fact that the universe is the place it is because physical objects attract each other (with a force which is directly proportional to their masses and inversely proportional to the square of the distance between those masses). It is not the case that this 'thing' called the Force of Gravity is constantly hard at work making sure that physical objects stick together in an orderly way. It is just a way of describing reality as it is in one of its physical aspects.

In exactly the same way God, as understood by Humanistic Christians, is a way of describing how the universe works in its spiritual/psychological/emotional aspect: for example, the fact that in doing good to others we receive benefits for ourselves, and that in forgiving others for their misdeeds we experience forgiveness for our own. In his *Religion in the Making*, A. N. Whitehead articulated this concept powerfully when he wrote:

God is that function in the world by reason of which our purposes are directed to ends which in our own consciousness are impartial as to our own interests. He is that element in life in virtue of which judgment stretches beyond facts of existence to values of existence. He is that element in virtue of which our purposes extend beyond values for ourselves to values for others. He is that element in virtue of which the attainment of such a value for others transforms itself into value for ourselves.

Unfortunately for many people, whether or not their concept of God embraces any or all of the abstract ethical principles discussed above, their concept also includes abstractions which have no place in the Humanistic Christian's concept of God. Prominent among these is the idea of God as a physically existing being. To think and talk about God as 'our father' can be helpful in reminding us that parent-child relationships at their best have a spiritual quality about them, but only if we remember that when we use that language we are speaking metaphorically.[23] Few outside that branch of the Christian Church which rejoices in the name 'The Church of Jesus Christ of Latter Day Saints', the Mormons as they are commonly known, will share the belief of its nineteenth-century founder, Joseph Smith, that 'God the Father has a body of flesh and bones'. This 13 million strong Mormon Church is more than a fringe sect. In the United States, it is, with its 5.5 million members, the fourth largest individual Christian denomination.

Although Joseph Smith, and others of his ilk have been unusual in boldly stating their belief that God is essentially an invisible human being, such a view probably lurks unconsciously in the background of many mainstream Christians.[24] Whilst it is probably fairly easy for most people to realise that when God is spoken about as 'our father' and Jesus as 'the shepherd of his flock' those statements are to be understood as metaphors (even if they have never heard the word metaphor in their lives before), but when they are constantly exposed in statements of the

Christian message (in sermons, prayers, hymns, and such like) to phrases such as 'God commands us to …', 'God is pleased when …', 'God can see …', 'God will help us if …' and other anthropomorphic statements made by people who claim to have some authority in the Christian Church, many people will come to think of such assertions as literal statements of fact. In the next chapter, I go on to consider some of the abstractions, influenced by the idea of God as a person, which are included in the concept of God of many Christians, and which cause those with a strong sense of what is right and good for human beings, people who have a deep awareness of the spiritual depths of life, to reject the whole concept of God as at best an irrelevance, and at worst as a destructive element in the lives of those who seek maximum happiness for themselves and others.

Chapter 4

What God is Not

Religion is by no means necessarily good. It may be very evil.
It may be the last resort of human savagery.
– Alfred North Whitehead. *Religion in the Making*

Some of the abstractions incorporated into the concept of God of some Christians add nothing of value to the collection of abstractions we derive from the ethical principles embedded in Jesus' teaching, and some are viciously destructive of the potential of Christianity to make the world a better place; some of those extraneous abstractions of course fall somewhere between those two extremes. In this chapter, I shall deal with what I regard as the most damaging ideas that have no place in the concept of God espoused by Humanistic Christians.

It is a striking fact that all these abstractions reflect the presence of authoritarian thinking, and it is doubtless the presence of such attitudes in their personalities which has guided the nervous systems of some people to select abstractions of this type as characteristics of God, whom they regard as the ultimate authority in the universe.

In using the term 'authoritarian' it is important to distinguish between the meaning of that word and the meaning of 'authoritative'. An authoritative statement is one which derives the authority which we recognise in it from the intrinsic value of the ideas expressed in it. An authoritarian statement is one where the person making that statement uses their status in some power hierarchy to try to force us to accept the truth of what they are saying because of their positional power. Encountering authoritative statements helps us towards acquiring valuable knowledge. This is not the case with authoritarian statements.

Unless we have been totally intimidated by growing up under the control of people who have had no respect for our unique individuality, authoritarian statements arouse a biologically-based rebellious determination to 'be our own person', and not to accept any ideas about any aspect of life just because someone tries to force us to accept them.

God as the creator of the universe

The Nicene Creed, which has for centuries been regarded as the official statement of orthodox Christian belief, was not developed because of any perceived religious or spiritual need on the part of the early Christian Church. It was cobbled together under pressure from the militaristic Roman Emperor Constantine in 325 CE.

Constantine, early in his reign had co-opted the growing Christian Church as an ally in pursuit of his political objectives, but became concerned that the increasingly splintered factions within that church were in danger of becoming a dangerous source of instability in his empire. The formulation of the Nicene Creed took place at a meeting of all the major Christian leaders of the day at Nicaea, in what is today north-western Turkey, and the conclusions reached were agreed to by all but two of the 318 delegates present. It is to be noted that the finished product resulting from those discussions, the Nicene Creed, contains not one word about the ethical principles urged upon us by Jesus, and that it came into existence only because of Constantine's perceived need for the Christian Church to be a powerful organisation which would present a strong united front in support of himself when needed, in return for the considerable patronage he had bestowed upon it.

The creed starts with the bold and unambiguous statement, 'I believe in God, the Father almighty, creator of heaven and earth, and of all things visible and invisible'. The further claim is often made by those Christians who believe this to be true, that God is the sustainer of the universe, implying that the universe only continues to exist because God is keeping it all together – that if he relaxed his grip on it, the universe would somehow disintegrate – it would cease to be. Although these days, particularly since the failure of the prophecies that the start of the new millennium would mark 'the end of the world', the idea of the universe ceasing to be does not receive as much attention from Christian proselytisers as it has sometimes done in the past, the idea that God in some way 'sustains' the universe still lurks somewhere in the minds of many Christians today. For others of us the idea that the universe only continues to exist because of the grace and favour of some almighty being who sustains it, and who could, and very probably will bring it all to an end when he has had enough of it, is quite preposterous.

Those who believe that God created the universe often feel they have scientific support for their position because of the very wide publicity which has been given to the 'Big Bang' theories developed by some of those Physicists and Applied Mathematicians whose professional scientific activities involve issues related to the origin of the universe. These 'Big Bang' cosmologists have succeeded in constructing a mathematical model which successfully accounts for the development of the universe from a point more than 13 billion years ago up to the present. Working backwards from the present, however, the mathematical model encounters what is technically known as a singularity, at which point the mathematics grinds to a halt.

Contrary to popular perception, however, there is not complete consensus among experts in the field as to which of the slightly variant Big Bang theories or other very different competing cosmological theories that have been developed is most likely to be closest to the truth. Until recently, however, it was Big Bang theories which seem to have made all the running, and many of those who have found one or other of those most convincing seem to believe, or have believed that the singularity the mathematics of the theory contains marks the start of the universe.

It is important to realise that any Big Bang theory of the start of the universe is a **theory**, and not an established fact. Although the mathematics which describes the evolution of the physical properties of the universe from a point 13.8 billion years ago down to the present time cannot be seriously faulted, identifying the singularity which occurs when we insert a value of t=0 (the value of the time variable at 'the start of the universe') into the equations of the model, as marking 'the start of the universe', is a purely speculative philosophical interpretation of what the impotence of the mathematical model to go further back in time means. Neither the maths, nor the physics of Big Bang theory has anything to say about the meaning to be attached to that singularity. It does not necessarily mean that the universe started at that point, and even less does it mean that time started at that point (as Stephen Hawking has asserted[25]). Neither does it mean, of course, that the universe did not start at that point. For the present at least, the question of when (if ever) the universe began is not one which either science or religion has anything authoritative to say about.

The second point that it is important to note in respect of any support Big Bang theory is believed to give to the idea that God created the universe, is that a number of increasingly sophisticated theories have been developed and are being developed at the moment which seem to at least have the potential to topple Big Bang theories from their pre-eminent position in the cosmological field. Given the continuously evolving nature of scientific thinking, advertising the correctness of any article of religious belief as supported by any currently fashionable interpretation of a scientific theory is a risky business.

So is that the end of the matter? I think not, and that it is worth looking a little more deeply at the belief that 'God, the Father Almighty' is the 'maker of heaven and earth'. Far from science (through Big Bang theory) offering any support for the idea that God is the creator of the universe, could it be that the relationship is the other way round – that the identification of a mathematical singularity with the origin of the universe by some intellectuals has come about because it fits in with, and gives support to the widely accepted religiously-based idea (conscious or unconscious) that God created the universe? For the present at least, we have no way of knowing which if either of these views most accurately reflects the true situation. All that we can say is that the respect accorded Big Bang theory by many cosmologists does not in any way prove that 'God created the universe'.

If there is no scientific support for that opening statement of the Christian Nicene Creed, why does the idea that it is true persist so strongly in the minds of so many Christians (and a great many other religious believers)? I would suggest that there are several factors at play here.

For one thing, co-opting one of the most impressive achievements of theoretical physical science as support for at least part of the Nicene Creed probably creates in some Christians a comforting, albeit totally erroneous belief that 'Science' has proved the truth of Christian beliefs.

Secondly, with the single exception of the hypothesised creation of the universe, every act of creation involves a novel rearrangement of pre-existing elements. It does not involve the creation of something from nothing. The great scientist Isaac Newton once modestly, but honestly and accurately said of his huge achievements in the fields of mathematics and physics, 'If I have seen further it is by standing on the shoulders of giants.' That is true of Newton's creations, but equally true of all creations in every sphere of life, not just in Science but, for example, in music and the visual and literary arts, in sport, in business, and in procreation. That part of creation which consists of the breathtaking marvel of ordinary human beings did not 'just happen' out of the blue. Our human origins lie in the penetration of a female ovum by a male sperm. All the constituent parts making up each of us were present in embryonic form before we existed. The act of sexual intercourse just brought certain crucial parts of our parents into close physical proximity with each other in such a way that they were able to interact with each other to create a new human life. We didn't come into existence in a vacuum.

When we talk about the 'creation' of the universe, Christian apologists, and other religious people are not talking about that creation as consisting of a novel rearrangement of existing elements, but as creation *ex nihilo* – from nothing: literally the bringing into existence of all that is in a vacuum. This is radically different from every other instance of creation we can think of, and applying the same name to it hides the striking fact that that when we are talking about God creating all that is, we are talking about something very different from what we are talking about in every other instance of creation. This immediately puts God and his creation out of the realm of ordinary human experience and bestows on them some sort of magical quality which it might be risky to question – we are after all then in the realm of the unknown, of the supernatural where even angels fear to tread and only a fool will rush in to involve him/herself with trying to understand something which it is beyond the ability of the human mind to grasp.

For some religious people such fears are real, as is the fear that if we do attempt to push the boundaries of our knowledge too far there is a serious danger that God might see us as trying to challenge him in some way, and this might make him angry, with potentially disastrous consequences for us if that were to happen. As the Genesis myth of humankind's expulsion from the Garden of Eden asserts, seeking to be as wise as God (Genesis 3:5-6) is something to be avoided at all costs.

For some of us the idea of anything coming into existence 'out of nothing' is just a nonsense. As Ludovic Kennedy said, in his book *All in the Mind: a Farewell to God*, 'To say that 'God' created this immensity out of nothing insults the imagination and adds nothing to the store of human knowledge.'[26] In fact if one can clear one's mind for a while of preconceived religious clutter, it is far easier to envisage the universe as a continuously changing something that has always existed, and always will exist, than that it came out of nowhere with a big bang and will probably one day disappear into nothing with another God-initiated big bang.

The more one's childhood experiences of family life were of an authoritarian system with one controlling person always at the head of it and laying down all the rules, rather than a democratic one in which people move in and out of leadership roles to secure the best match between the unique abilities of each family member and the moment by moment needs of the family, the more difficult one will find it to conceive of a system as huge as the universe operating successfully by mutual adjustment of its constituent parts without some controlling agent who resides outside the system in charge. The universe, however, is a self-organising system, and self-organising systems exhibit a design but do not necessarily have a designer who is located outside the system. Some aspects of the work undertaken in the relatively recently developed scientific field of Cybernetics, exploring the nature of control systems, are of great relevance to our understanding of this aspect of the universe.

To discard the notion of the universe as **created by God** does not mean discarding the concept of God as obsolete or irrelevant – it just means revising our understanding of his/her/its nature, realising that God is not something external to the universe who operates upon it as he pleases, but is rather an integral part of the whole universe, of all that is[27] – that he/she/it is a property of the universe, the property which captures the idea that Good is ultimately stronger than Evil, and that in helping others to live a better and happier life we gain benefits for ourselves that we can acquire in no other way.

God as 'our Lord', a Ruler, a King, a Man of War who is to be praised, worshipped, and sometimes, when we feel we have done wrong and displeased him, to be grovelled before.

Once God is seen as the creator and controller of the universe, what more natural than to ascribe kingly qualities to this being, and to see ourselves as his must-be-loyal subjects, or else …?

But of course God is no ordinary king. Given his unlimited power and knowledge he must be more extremely kingly than any mere human king, and so what more fitting title for him than King of kings, and Lord of lords. Anything humans can do, God can do better. And so, just as it has been so important to an earthly king that his subjects be loyal to him, and accept his authority and their own subordinate status, we take it for granted that God 'expects' the same attitude from us towards him. We therefore are at pains to show him how we glory in his greatness, basking in his reflected glory, and far from challenging it, feel that we must constantly reassure him that we regard ourselves as pretty worthless, 'miserable sinners' rotten at the core, who will do all we can to promote his much superior image and reputation. So we set aside times of prayer and communal activity to 'worship' him and tell him how great he is.

The Old Testament Book of Psalms, very largely absorbed with particular affection into 'Services of Worship' in the Christian Church, is instructive in this regard. The recurrent theme throughout that book of an urging of us to 'Praise the Lord' builds in a powerful crescendo in the last five Psalms in that book (everyone of which starts with the words 'Praise ye the Lord'), culminating in a jubilant outburst in the last Psalm (number 150), the first verse of which begins, and the last verse of which ends with the words, 'Praise ye the Lord', with every verse between these two containing a twofold instruction to, 'Praise him', and specifying how and why this is to be done: 'for his mighty acts' and 'according to his excellent greatness', 'with the sound of the trumpet', 'with the psaltery and harp', 'with the timbrel and dance', 'with stringed instruments and organs', and 'upon the loud cymbals' and 'the high sounding cymbals'.

This attitude of almost unbearably utter devotion and gratitude, so brilliantly caricatured by John Cleese acting as the school chaplain in the Monty Python film *The Meaning of Life* ('Oh God, you **are wonderful!**'), seems to be widespread among authoritarian Christians. Such revelling in authoritarian submission to a being possessed of unlimited 'power and might' is probably the aspect of the traditional Christian concept of God which stokes the fires of militant atheism of the Richard Dawkins variety most vigorously. But it is the antithesis of the attitude expressed by Jesus throughout his teaching, and has no place in the concept of God espoused by Humanistic Christians.[28] In the words of one anonymous, enlightened priest, God is 'beyond the vulgarities of praise and power.'

Seeking to be powerful and associating with those who were held no attractions for Jesus. His lack of social climbing ambitions led him to be ridiculed in some quarters as a mere 'friend of publicans and sinners', while his feelings about our seeking for ourselves the same prestige as is afforded powerful political and religious figures is well illustrated in his statement reported in verse 26 of the twentieth chapter of Matthew's gospel, 'Whoever wishes to be great among you must be your servant.' The fact that those sentiments are repeated at least five times elsewhere in Matthew and in the gospels of Mark and Luke suggests that this way of looking at what constitutes greatness was deeply ingrained in Jesus' thinking and became so in the memories of his disciples. What is reported in Luke 22:26 makes this even clearer, 'I am among you as one who serves.' This makes the Church's almost universal preference for the version of the so-called Lord's Prayer to be found in Matthew 6:9-13 singularly inappropriate. In this version the words, 'Thine be the kingdom, the power and the glory' are appended to the prayer as it is reported in Luke 11:2-4.

But there is a further very important consideration which is a powerful motivator of the rejection by humanistically-oriented Christians of the concept of God as 'our Lord', our Royal Ruler.

It is only relatively recently in the history of the Judaic and Christian religions that where kings have existed they have not all been leading figures in their country's military adventures. Although there have always been those in Jewish religion who have not been happy with the situation, in that part of Jewish religious literature incorporated into the Christian Bible as its 'Old Testament', the theme of God as a warrior king is often conspicuous. To quote but one example, 'The Lord is a man of war ... thy right hand, O Lord, hath dashed in pieces the enemy ... Who is like unto thee, O Lord, among the gods? Who is like thee, glorious in holiness, fearful in praises, doing wonders?' (Exodus 15:3, 6, and 11). Verse 21 of that same chapter ('the horse and his rider hath he thrown into the sea') doubtless refers to one of those wonders, the occasion when God showed his strength in protecting the fleeing children of Israel by drowning the pursuing horse-mounted army of Pharaoh in the Red Sea. Believing that there exists a controlling ultimate power and authority in the universe who behaves in such a callous and cruel way is totally incompatible with any commitment to the ethical principles urged upon us by Jesus.

The Old Testament book of Joshua is particularly rich in examples of the concept of God as a terrifying force with a blood lust, but there are plenty of examples of that elsewhere in the Old Testament. One that should not be overlooked is verse 35 of chapter 19 of the Second Book of Kings, where we are told that:

That very night the angel of the Lord set out and struck down one hundred eighty-five thousand in the camp of the Assyrians; when morning dawned they were all dead bodies.

Presumably the 'angel of the Lord' who carried out this mass slaughter had his Lord's (our Lord's?) approval for his, on this special occasion, breaking one of God's own 'Ten Commandments', **'Thou shalt not kill'** (Exodus 20:13 and Deuteronomy 5:17). Or perhaps God's commandments do not apply to himself and his 'angels'?

The ideas of God as a king, and a man of war, have no place in the concept of God of Humanistic Christians. Of all the qualities some Christians sometimes ascribe to God which most thoroughly contradict the concept implicit in Jesus' teachings, this is the most blatant. The many Christians who subscribe to it, (and their numbers go up dramatically when their own country is involved in a war), have simply uncritically taken over the Old Testament concept of God as a warrior king who is constantly fighting for the welfare of 'his people' against the forces of darkness. It is not for nothing that Onward Christian Soldiers is one of the best-known Christian hymns, with its rousing chorus of,

Onward Christian soldiers,
Marching as to war.
With the Cross of Jesus
Going on before.

Horrors! What a terrible distortion of the 'Love your enemies,' and 'Gentleness is stronger than violence' message of the life and teachings of Jesus. His rebuke to the sword-wielding member of the group who was with him when he was arrested in the Garden of Gethsemane, 'Put your sword back into its place; for all who take the sword will perish by the sword,' will not be most authoritarian Christians' favourite New Testament quote, and those words of Jesus were presumably not in St Paul's mind when in his first epistle to the Corinthians, he asserts, in verses 16 and 17 of Chapter 3, 'If any man defile the temple of God, him shall God destroy', nor when a little later in that same epistle, in respect of a (to his mind) particularly scandalous bit of sexual misbehaviour, he tells the Corinthian Church that they must 'hand this man over to Satan for the destruction of the flesh' (I Corinthians 5:5). Nor, presumably, were they in the minds of those 'devout Christians' George Bush and Tony Blair when they initiated and supported the unleashing of 'shock and awe' military tactics to topple the cruel regime of Saddam Hussein in Iraq, a way of handling that horrendous situation which has been an unmitigated disaster for so many ordinary citizens in that part of the world ever since.

To those of us who believe that gentleness really is ultimately stronger than violence, the extent to which a major Christian leader, a proclaimed Christian saint, has preached violence as the right method to deal with wrongdoing is positively alarming. Warnings to the churches about the 'wrath and fury' of God (Romans 2: 5-8, for example), and in the next verse about the 'tribulation and anguish' they will have to endure if they do wrong, are to be found scattered throughout Paul's letters to young churches. And such references to God as a brutal punitive force in the world are not restricted to just the writings of Paul. Although entitled, in the New Revised Standard Version of the English Bible, 'The Second Letter of Paul to the Thessalonians', the weight of modern scholarly opinion is that that epistle was not written by Paul, unlike the first epistle to that young church, which most probably was. Whoever it was who wrote the second epistle rivals Paul for the vehemence with which he projects his sadism onto God:

> … in flaming fire, inflicting vengeance on those who do not know God and on those who do not obey the gospel of our Lord Jesus. These will suffer the punishment of eternal destruction, separated from the presence of the Lord and from the glory of his might (II Thessalonians 1:8-9).

This aggressively warlike approach to the reform of wrongdoers is in sharp contrast to the judgement of General Eisenhower, who as supreme commander of the victorious Allied Forces in the Second World War, was probably the most powerful military leader the world has seen since the time of Alexander the Great (the fourth-century BCE Greek king whose prowess on the battlefield earned him the title of 'Lord of Asia'), that, 'You do not lead by hitting people over the head – that's assault, not leadership.' What this says about St Paul's qualification to be treated with uncritical respect as a major thought-leader within Christianity ought to provoke serious discussion among adherents to that religion. As things stand, it is hardly surprising that the Christian Church has not only been largely impotent to put an end to war, but has even from time to time given its support to, and often initiated 'Holy wars'. No wonder that the twentieth-century English poet and novelist Thomas Hardy could, in a little poem entitled *Christmas 1924*, write bitterly,

"Peace upon earth," the angels sang.
We pay a thousand priests to ring it.
And after 2000 years of Mass
We've got as far as poison gas.

The God of Authoritarian Christianity may be a man of war, but for those who identify with the idea of Humanistic Christianity such a concept has no place in a Christian concept of God.

The hypothesised fundamentally adversarial relationship which exists between God and humankind

The demand for subservience by rank and file church members to the higher authority of their leaders is frequently seen as the embodiment on the purely human level of the relationship believed (by those whose Christianity is of the authoritarian type), to exist between humans and God. As is the case in all authoritarian systems, an adversarial relationship between the ruler and those they rule is part and parcel of the organisational structure of which they are a part. Conflict is inevitable where an adversarial relationship exists, and in the case of authoritarian Christianity that conflict is between being 'good' and obedient to 'God's will' (as formulated for us by church leaders) and committing sins, i.e. doing things of which church leaders disapprove. The more behaviours that are forbidden (and Christians differ widely among themselves about exactly what behaviours are permitted and which are not), the more sins will be committed. For those who subscribe to the tenets of authoritarian Christianity, life is a constant conflict between their wills and what they have been persuaded to regard as God's will – an energy-wasting activity which makes many people's lives considerably less happy than they might otherwise have been.

The very different non-adversarial relationship with God which Humanistic Christians feel they have, is well illustrated by the story which is told of the old Quaker who on his deathbed was asked by a more conservatively religious friend if he had 'made his peace' with his maker. To this the old man responded, 'I didn't know we had ever quarrelled.'

The fundamental wickedness of humankind

The most striking characteristic, and indeed the defining property of an authoritarian organisation is the power differentials that exist within it. In so far as any organisation is a democratic one, there is a free flow of knowledge and influence among members. Everyone is entitled to have their say, and thereby to influence to at least some degree the outcome of decision-making within the group.

To the extent that any organisation is an authoritarian one there is no such freedom. The greatest virtue demanded of rank and file members is not constructive creativity and contributions to deeper insight and understanding, but obedience to the dictates of the Top Dogs in the organisation, and those Top Dogs who seek to retain control in their own hands will have learnt as they worked their way up to their current position of power and influence how best to disable any attempts to challenge their authority. Probably the most effective way to minimise any such challenges is to undermine the self-confidence and feelings of self-worth of those who might have the temerity to challenge their leaders at any point in the future.

Many authoritarian Christian leaders have been guilty of doing this on a horrendous scale. Completely ignoring the strong statement in the very first chapter of the Bible (which when it suits them they regard as containing nothing but absolute truth) to the effect that, 'God saw everything that he had made, and indeed, it was very good' (Genesis 1:31), they have taken every opportunity to try to make adherents to their religion feel bad about themselves – that they are miserable sinners, unworthy to come into the divine presence without the intervention of some mediating presence such as 'God's son' or perhaps God's son's 'mother' – the Virgin Mary. And those Christian leaders who think, and/or have thought in this way have not been slow to take advantage of the opportunity to position themselves as the indispensable managers of such mediating contact.

One of the most ridiculous ideas which they have concocted to undermine humanity's self-confidence has been that of Original Sin – the idea that because of the disobedience of some extremely remote ancestors of ours (Adam and Eve) we are all of us born as sinners who need forgiveness from God for being born as such. The fact that this theory is directly contradicted by a verse in the biblical book of Ezekiel (Verse 20 of Chapter 18) where it is unambiguously stated that, 'A child shall not suffer for the iniquity of a parent, nor a parent suffer for the iniquity of a child', seems to be an issue which is never faced by those fundamentalist authoritarian Christians who generally grant even the most preposterous statements the status of absolute truths if they appear in the Bible. The position of Christian doctrine in regard to Original Sin is even further complicated by the statement God is reported to have made in expounding the Ten Commandments (in Exodus 20:6 and Deuteronomy 5:9) that, 'I the Lord your God am a jealous God, punishing children for the iniquity of parents, to the third and fourth generation'. Interestingly the words 'Original Sin' do not occur in the New Testament.

As I suggest in my *The Two Faces of Christianity*, anxiety about our sexual appetites is probably what really lies at the root of orthodox Christian belief about disobedience being the 'original sin' of humanity. That theory is almost certainly a rationalisation of sexual anxiety, a rationalisation which is particularly comforting to those of an authoritarian cast of mind within the Church: it justifies efforts to curb and control the sexual behaviour of humanity. The psalmist's lament (in verses 3 and 5 of Psalm 51) that, 'in sin did my mother conceive me', and 'my sin is ever before me' is just the tip of the iceberg of the Christian Church's discomfort with the fact that our sexual desires intrude themselves into our consciousness as often as they do.

The idea of original sin, to the discussion of which the former Roman Catholic, and now Anglican priest Matthew Fox has made an invaluable and enlightening contribution in his book *Original Blessing*, is the foundational belief upon which that central defining doctrine of authoritarian Christianity, the barbaric dogma of the Atonement to which I now turn attention is based. This is a particularly objectionable bit of very human psychopathology.

The necessity for punishment of wrongdoing

One of the minor, and yet important life experiences which I think has shaped my concern about the damage that authoritarian thinking and behaviour has done to human beings occurred when I was still at school. I attended one of the Marist

Brothers high schools for a couple of years, something which was educationally, intellectually and socially a disaster. Non-Catholics like myself attended a special 'Bible Study' class while the Catholic pupils attended their daily 'catechism class'. One day the Catholic brother who took our Bible Study class thought of asking everyone how their parents punished them when they had done wrong. I found that a somewhat odd question, and when it came to my turn to speak I said, 'I don't think my parents ever do punish me.' My reply caused a considerable hubbub. 'What?' said the Catholic brother. 'Do you mean you can do whatever you like?' and shook his head in bewilderment when I replied that I didn't think there was anything I wanted to do that my parents would disapprove of. That event was, I think, the first time I had come face to face with the centrality of the concept of punishment in the lives of so many people.

To my adult mind, the totally untrue belief that it is only punishment and the threat of it which prevents human social relations from descending into anarchy has done a huge amount of harm to the human race. That harm intensified when it entered into religious thinking. Although not restricted to Christianity it is its corrupting effect within that religion which is of most concern to me in this book, and I shall restrict my attention to that subject here.

Before proceeding further, let us note that there are two different sorts of situation to which the term punishment is applied. Psychologists use the word punishment to describe any situation in which a particular behaviour is followed by an unpleasant state of affairs, either physically or psychologically unpleasant, or both. One type of punishment is what happens to us when we disregard the realities of nature. If we blithely step off the roof of a tall building believing that we shall land comfortably on our feet, nature is likely to punish us with an extremely unpleasant consequence for our disregard of one of the facts about 'the way the universe is'. If we eat or drink any substance we come across without establishing that it is safe for human consumption, nature will inevitably sooner or later punish us for our carelessness with some violent illness or even death. Such types of punishment are not willed upon us by another human being: they are just the inevitable consequence of disregard of some aspect of reality. That sort of punishment will always be with us, not because any human or divine being visits it upon us, but just because that is 'the way things are'.

Very different is the sort of punishment which one human being deliberately inflicts on another because of their disapproval of something in that other person's behaviour. This sort of punishment is never necessary and inevitable – there is always a better way of modifying someone's behaviour when we feel that needs to be done – it just needs some psychological skill, and sometimes the resources to implement that better approach. There is a great deal of truth in the old proverbs to the effect that, 'More people are flattered into virtue than are bullied out of vice', and 'Punishment does much, but encouragement does more'.

Unfortunately the traditional Christian concept of God was developed over many centuries when psychological knowledge was minimal, and punishment must have often seemed to be a necessity in curbing and preventing 'bad behaviour'. If one holds that belief, then any anthropomorphically-conceived Supreme Being would inevitably have to use punishment as one of the tools at its disposal to ensure a reasonably well-ordered world.

Probably all the most oppressive, frightening, and anti-life concepts with which large parts of the Christian Church have been destructively encumbered can be traced back to a belief in the necessity for those in any sort of authority to punish those who do not accept their authority. That belief became part and parcel of the concept of God which developed long before the appearance of Jesus on the scene, and was simply uncritically accepted by Christians as their religion developed.

And so the authoritarian branch of mainstream Christianity still cherishes the concept of Hell, and, contradictorily, that most appalling segment of Christian theology – the theory of the Atonement. That theory (or dogma as it is usually called) about the significance of the crucifixion of Jesus, states that 'God' ordained the torture and death of his 'dearly beloved son' as a substitute punishment for all the sins of humanity. It is an example of the sadomasochistic psychopathology which is strongly present in the thinking of those subscribers to the authoritarian branch of Christianity who wallow in the gory details of the crucifixion. The origins of this blasphemous idea most probably lie in the ambivalent attitudes some fathers have towards the growing strength, success and attractiveness of their sons as they grow older, in contrast with their own declining powers. Projecting their hostility towards youth onto God gives some people a feeling that the negative side of their ambivalent feelings for their children is just part of 'the way things are' – even God has such feelings.

Such a punishment-based idea, and the concept of God from which it springs have no part in Humanistic Christianity. I discuss this and related issues in some depth in Chapter 6 of my *The Two Faces of Christianity*.

The almost (but not quite) universal acceptance by Christians of the idea that belief in the truth of the Dogma of the Atonement lies at the heart of 'what it means to be a Christian' is one part of 'The Trouble with Christianity'. Not only is that Dogma a completely internally inconsistent muddle in terms of the biblical authority which it is supposed to have, but the endless pleas to God to 'be merciful to us miserable sinners' with which many Christian Church services are saturated makes no sense if it is true that, as stated in the Epistle of John, Chapter 2, verse 2, 'He is the propitiation for our sins: and not for ours only, but also for the sins of the whole world', and if Paul is not deluded in the belief he confidently asserts in II

Corinthians (5:14), that referring to the death of Jesus, 'We are convinced that one died for all'.

If those statements are true, then mercy doesn't come into it – there is nothing to be merciful about. One can almost imagine an anthropomorphically-conceived God responding to yet another batch of pleas for him to 'show mercy' with an exasperated, 'For goodness sake stop worrying about your eternal future, and stop worrying me to show mercy on you. You humans are indeed a bad lot, and do indeed deserve to suffer for all eternity, but as I've told you over and over again, because of the pain, sufferings and death which at my behest my son suffered on your behalf I have forgiven you all. Now go away and get real.'

The antagonism to pleasure
Closely related to the idea of the necessity for punishment and the sadomasochistically-inspired glorification of pain and suffering, is the attitude of authoritarian Christianity towards people enjoying themselves. For many outside the fold of the Christian Church (and even for some within it), that Church is a real Mother Grundy when it comes to the enjoyment of pleasure, that quality which Albert Schweitzer very appropriately partially defined as the 'mysterious exaltation of the will-to-live'.

St Paul's extensive writings have been influential in this respect. The authorship of more than half of the 27 books of the New Testament are (or have been in some parts of the Church) attributed to Paul, and to judge from those writings the only pleasure he allowed himself to indulge in was the pleasure of enduring the physical suffering which was inflicted on him because of his religious convictions by various political authorities. Certainly direct sexual pleasure was an absolute no-no for Paul, and he did not hold back on vigorous attempts to persuade those whose spiritual welfare he saw as his special responsibility from indulging in any bodily pleasures.

I appeal to you therefore, brothers and sisters, by the mercies of God, to present your bodies as a living sacrifice, holy and acceptable to God, which is your spiritual worship (Romans 12:1).

At times his anti-sex stance could be completely over the top.

Those who belong to Christ Jesus have crucified the flesh with its passions and desires (Galatians 5:24).

At no point in his epistles did Paul ever try to provide any rational argument as to why sexual self-denial should be a Christian virtue, and 'acceptable to God'. Again, a much fuller discussion of this topic is to be found in my *The Two Faces of Christianity*.

Paul is by no means the only Christian leader to have campaigned against the enjoyment of pleasure – St Augustine and Cardinal Newman amongst others have been outspoken on the subject, and it is by no means only sexual pleasure of which much of the Christian Church has given the impression that part of its message to the world is, 'You are not in this world to enjoy yourself. You are here to do God's will.' As long ago as 256 CE an 'Ordinance' was issued by one of the synodal gatherings of the early Christian Church, the 'Second Council of Carthage', to the effect that, 'If any clerk or monk utters jocular words causing laughter, let him be excommunicated', and more than a hundred years before that Clemens of Alexandria, a second-century leader of one of the splintered factions of Christianity at that time, had written, 'Laughter does not become a Christian'.

One important source of pleasure for many of us is the contemplation of the beautiful – the beautiful in nature, in art, and in the realm of ideas. If pleasure is regarded as undesirable for the development of our spiritual life, beautiful things are likely to be regarded as suspect. This may be part of the reason why so many of the non-conformist Protestant Churches have often conducted their services in buildings which, if not downright ugly are architecturally drab and uninspiring to be in.

Christianity is certainly a religion of extremes where beauty is concerned. Some of the greatest musical masterpieces have been created for use within some branches of the Christian Church, and particularly within the Anglican Churches one can often hear musical performances of the very highest quality. For sheer aesthetic beauty the Evensong services in some Cathedrals and University College Chapels would be hard to beat. But the music in Christian church services is often of the most appalling quality, with beauty nowhere to be heard or seen.

Much the same goes for Christian literature, amongst which some magnificent writing is to be found, but also much in which the creation of beauty seems to have been the last thing on the writer's or translator's mind.

Beauty is not a dispensable luxury so far as spirituality is concerned. Inspired thinkers have for centuries explored what they believed to be a close relationship between Goodness, Beauty, and Truth.

One of the most thought-provoking pieces of writing I have come across as to why we should not neglect our exposure to beautiful things in our religious life, is contained in Alexander Solzhenitsyn's acceptance speech for his Nobel Prize for Literature in 1970.[29] In it he said,

Perhaps, then, the old trinity of Truth, Goodness and Beauty is not simply the dressed-up, worn-out old formula we in our presumptuous, materialistic youth thought it was. If the crowns of these three trees meet (as most scholars have asserted) and if the too obvious, too straight sprouts of Truth and Goodness have been knocked down, cut off, not let grow – perhaps the whimsical, unpredictable, unexpected branches of Beauty will work their way through, rise up to that very place, and thus complete the work of all three.

The Latin motto, 'Pulchritudo splendor veritatis' – 'Beauty is the splendour of truth' sends us a similar message about one aspect of the inter-relationships between goodness, beauty, and truth.

One of the 'troubles with Christianity' is that so many of its activities are pursued without regard for the power of beauty to put us in touch with deep spiritual realities. In doing this the Church is reducing its acceptability to those people for whom enjoying beautiful things is an important part of the pleasure they get out of life.

Guilt, temptation, and the Devil

The thinking of those who subscribe to the beliefs of Authoritarian Christianity is riddled with guilt, and the Church in general has encouraged at least confession of one's wrong-doing, of one's sins, as a healing mechanism for the pain and worry that guilt causes. That process can bring some relief, but it is usually short-lived because at least the temptation 'to sin' will inevitably always be present, and the more of an issue the Church makes of it, the stronger that temptation will be. As the American humourist Samuel Langhorne Clemens, best known by his pseudonym Mark Twain, once said, 'We were little Christian children who had early been taught the value of forbidden fruit.'

A different sort of technique, which is also for most people only partially successful, is to fasten onto the idea of 'the devil', rather than one's own mind as the source of wicked thoughts and evil desires. The fundamental motivation for all human behaviour is the desire to feel good about oneself, and we sometimes go to great lengths to avoid becoming aware of anything in our minds that makes us feel that we are not as good as we like to think we are. Sigmund Freud, the early twentieth-century neurologist and father of Psychoanalysis was the first person to look systemati-cally at the defence mechanisms we use in order to avoid becoming aware of aspects of ourselves that we wish were not there. These defence mechanisms are things like Repression, Denial, Projection, Reaction Formation, Intellectualisation, and Rationalisation.

One of Freud's early followers was the Swiss Psychiatrist Carl Gustav Jung (until Freud's neurotic authoritarian personality proved too much for him). Taking up some of Freud's Defence Mechanism ideas, Jung formulated the idea that, in addition to the aspects of ourselves which we show to the world (our Persona, as he called it), we all carry a Shadow Self, which as far as possible we keep tucked away out of sight of both the world and ourselves. Into this Shadow Self we push as many of the characteristics of ourselves which we do not like as possible. We don't want the world to see them, and very often we don't even want to see them ourselves. These characteristics are denied and repressed but cannot thereby be got rid of. They are parts of ourself, albeit for the most part unconscious parts.

Despite our best efforts, our Shadow Self does intrude itself from time to time into our daily lives, causing us when we become aware of it, to exclaim things like, 'Where did that come from? It's not like me to say (or do) things like that.' Examples of this are the sudden eruption of strong anger in someone who is normally very laid back and unruffled in their daily lives, and the 'hard as nails' individual who is suddenly moved to tears by someone's unexpectedly compassionate response to their harsh behaviour towards them.

The contents of our Shadow, if they are vigorously enough repressed, seem to be no part of ourselves when they do show themselves – they seem to belong to some invading force which has temporarily taken over control of our mind. This is how the concept of the existence of a devil has come about. Some people are so reluctant to own, and take responsibility for the darker shadow side of their minds, that when their shadow self erupts with uncharacteristic, and sometimes quite frighteningly unexpected behaviour, they interpret the phenomenon as one of 'devil possession' – an unhelpful way of looking at the situation, but one which has the inestimably useful benefit for those who use it, of relieving them of blame for their actions. 'It wasn't me. The devil made me do it.'

St Paul provides an early recorded example of the use of this strategy. In verses 18 to 20 of the seventh chapter of his Epistle to the Romans, Paul wrote:

For I know that nothing good dwells within me, that is, in my flesh. I can will what is right, but cannot do it. For I do not do the good I want but the evil I do not want is what I do. Now if I do what I do not want, it is no longer I that do it, but sin that dwells within me, therefore I am innocent.

From the perspective of Humanistic Christianity no one has anything to fear from admitting to themselves that they possess some qualities which they, and doubtless others, if they knew about them, would disapprove of, even be horrified by. No divine punishment awaits us in the next world for our shortcomings and faults. Whatever painful consequences we suffer for any of our wrongdoing takes place in this world because of the way relevant constituent parts of the universe respond to whatever it was we did or failed to do. Being honest with at least ourselves about our capacity for wrongdoing, and about the fact that from time to time we do things which we believe to be wrong, is the essential first step towards that degree of psychological maturity which will deepen our understanding and experience of spiritual truths, and help us to become better, kinder, more loving people.

Attitudes to parenting, contraception, homosexuality, euthanasia, and abortion

These five issues have a common thread running through them, attitudes to which sometimes sharply differentiate authoritarian Christians from their humanistic fellow-religionists.

Parenting

Authoritarian Christian parenting has made a major contribution to the amount of unhappiness there is in the world. That parenting style is frequently marked by envy of the young, the desire for control of other people (particularly of most aspects of their children's lives), a frequent lack of respect for the unique individuality of every child, the imposing of rigid rules and dispensing of punishment for infractions of them, emotional manipulation and the instilling of guilt as a control mechanism, and often physical abuse. 'Spare the rod and spoil the child'[30], those words beloved of many conservative Christians, must be one of the most unchristian and damaging psychopathological beliefs a parent can have about bringing up children. Destructive inner conflict, frustrated rage, and depression are often the lifelong companions of those who have had the misfortune to be brought up in this way.

The humanistic parenting style is very different. Such parents seek to influence the development of their children's attitudes and behaviour, rather than to control them. They really connect emotionally with their children, and through the way they themselves behave, inspire in their children the belief that one should never sacrifice a person to a principle – that if it comes to having to choose between behaving correctly according to some moral injunction and being kind, the truly Christian response is to choose to be kind. Such parents believe that arrogance ought never to manifest itself in their dealings with their children; that disagreements can almost always be solved by democratic discussion in an attempt to find a WIN-WIN resolution of any conflict, and that gentleness is ultimately more powerful than violence. Most importantly they treat a child's wrongdoing in a kindly non-punitive way, aimed at helping the child to learn from its mistakes better ways of being: they are slow to anger and quick to forgive.[31] In doing so their behaviour is in complete harmony with the response given by Jesus when he was asked which was 'the greatest commandment in the law' (Matthew 22:36, and Mark 22:12), in which he identified the urging of us to love God, and to love our neighbour as more fundamentally important than all the restrictive negative injunctions to refrain from various behaviours. This indicates very clearly his belief in the Power of the Positive – the superiority of encouraging good behaviour over punishing the bad.

Children brought up by parents who manifest these values in their behaviour towards their children will not necessarily grow up entirely problem-free, but they will certainly be happier children, and happier and more successful as adults than they would have been had they grown up under an authoritarian Christian regime. There is a rather lovely capturing of some of these ideas in a little anonymous poem, entitled, *Children Learn What They Live*:

If a child lives with criticism
He learns to condemn.
If a child lives with hostility
He learns to fight.
If a child lives with ridicule
He learns to be shy.
If a child lives with shame
He learns to feel guilty.
If a child lives with tolerance
He learns to be patient.
If a child lives with encouragement
He learns to be confident.
If a child lives with praise
He learns to appreciate.
If a child lives with fairness
He learns justice.
If a child lives with security
He learns to have faith.

If a child lives with approval
He learns to like himself.
If a child lives with acceptance
and friendliness
He learns to find love in the world.

Contraception

For all the sometimes hard and tiring work involved in being a parent, that privilege has for some of us provided the moments of deepest joy in our lives. By contrast, an unwanted pregnancy must be one of the most frightening and devastating situations that human beings, especially female human beings can get caught up in. One of the many huge benefits which the increasingly rapid developments in medical science has brought to mankind is the power it has given us to enjoy the pleasures of sex without the fear of being responsible for the initiation of an unwanted pregnancy. It is a sad reflection on how far human societies in general are from achieving a reasonable level of psychological maturity that so many people have little or no knowledge about, and access to contraceptive options.

One of the many blots on the reputation of the Christian Church is the blanket opposition many of those in its authoritarian branch have shown, often viciously, towards the use of contraception. There is absolutely no rational spiritual, religious, medical or psychological justification for the position many of them have taken in this matter, and not to do anything to prevent the birth of unwanted children when our planet is already grossly overburdened with an ever-increasing population which sooner or later it will be unable to support, is grossly irresponsible, anti-life, cruel, and unchristian.

For the Humanistic Christian, the negative attitude towards contraception which abounds in its authoritarian wing is totally unjustified and another example of the way in which that branch of the Christian Church has disregarded, and continues to disregard Jesus' powerfully humanistic principle of never sacrificing a person to a principle, which lies at the heart of his pronouncement that, 'The Sabbath was made for humankind, not humankind for the Sabbath.' (Mark 2:27).

Homosexuality

The violent opposition many branches of the Christian Church have shown to same sex relationships and marriages is another less than praiseworthy feature of Christianity, and one that is manifested much more commonly in those whose religion is of an authoritarian rather than of a humanistic type. Whether anyone finds that it is in a relationship with a man or with a woman that their desire for a close emotional and sexual relationship is best satisfied is not a matter of any spiritual significance whatsoever. And their preference in that matter is not determined by personal choice. Many people have been, and are caused immense distress if their sexual orientation is different from the approved pattern in the society in which they are living, but there is nothing they can do to change that orientation by sheer effort of will. Whether and when we engage in any sort of sexual behaviour with anyone – man or woman or just ourselves, is something which is under our control, but whether it is a man or a woman we are attracted to is not. That preference is determined by our psychobiological make-up (which is the result of a complex interaction between our genetic endowment and our early life experience), and there is nothing the individual can do about it except either admit or deny it to themselves.

Being attracted to someone who is of the same or a different sex from ourselves is neither a sin nor a Christian virtue – it is just the way things are. To moralistically judge and condemn someone the objects of whose sexual desires are different from our own is no more a Christian virtue than it would be to condemn anyone for being of above or below average height, or for having green eyes or blonde hair, and the extent to which those in high places within the Christian Church have pronounced judgement on those whose sexuality is not of the heterosexual type has led to a great deal of emotional dishonesty and lack of authenticity within the Church. A sensitive account of some of the sorts of suffering to which this has given rise within the Roman Catholic Church is to be found in Bernárd Lynch's book, *If It Wasn't Love: Sex, Death and God*. That book also contains the statement that, 'Gay priests, as is well reported and documented, constitute forty to fifty percent of Catholic clergy.'[32] The feeling that comes up when we hear some of the very emotional attacks on homosexuality within the Church that, 'the lady' (or more usually the gentleman) 'protesteth too much' may indeed often be well-founded.

Euthanasia

To deny to any human being the right to use all the benefits of modern medical science to terminate their life in a dignified and beautiful way when that life has become intolerable to them, is a cruel and heartless act for which there can be no acceptable religious justification. To the extent that the Christian Church has used its influence to prevent euthanasia being a freely available option to those who desire this form of medical help it has been blatantly disregarding the fundamental ethical principle of compassionate love which was at the heart of Jesus' thinking about what sort of attitudes and behaviours constitute the Kingdom of Heaven – the Kingdom of God. Humanistic Christians need to be more vocal than we often have been in the past in calling for not just the toleration of euthanasia, but the compassionate acceptance of it as a socially and spiritually much-needed way of allowing people the freedom to do what they passionately want to do to reduce the amount of suffering in the world.

Opposition to freely available euthanasia is not just ethically unacceptable to the Humanistic Christian; the religious opposition to it is deeply flawed. When that opposition is challenged, the justification for it is generally asserted to be something along the lines of, 'It is not for human beings to decide when it is the right time for someone to die. Only God can do that.' Not only is such a view totally unsupported by any evidence beyond the confident assertion of the believer in its truth, but that statement is meaningless except in terms of a 'Controlling Being' view of the Nature of God. Even more disastrously for that point of view, anyone who believes in it ought, to be consistent, to crusade against all forms of medical treatment, against all military activities, and be an implacable opponent of the death penalty. The fact that opponents of euthanasia are not famous for being either committed pacifists or opponents of the death penalty suggests that invoking the 'will of God' is just a fig-leaf to cover the less exalted and thoroughly unchristian belief that it is OK for humans to determine when someone must die as punishment for their wrongdoing, but not to make such a decision in the interests of relieving someone's suffering.

Abortion

Much the same general religious, ethical, and humanitarian principles apply to abortion as to contraception and euthanasia. The big difference between euthanasia and abortion is of course that abortion involves terminating a life when the possessor of that life has not requested such a termination. But to equate the experience of the 'being alive' of a foetus which possesses only the embryonic beginnings of a nervous system with the functioning nervous system of even the newborn is absurd. Aborting a pregnancy which has by no means yet reached full-term is unquestionably something very different from terminating the life of even the newborn, let alone someone who has been alive for many months or years.

Nevertheless aborting a foetus is undoubtedly a far more

potentially traumatic thing for a mother (and to some extent at least, for a father) to go through. What anyone who is weighing up their options in terms of having an abortion needs is generous sympathetic, helpful support for whatever they decide to do. The last thing they need is to be persecuted with the sort of guilt-inducing criticism and condemnation for which authoritarian Christians have so often been responsible. For the Humanistic Christian such behaviour is profoundly unchristian. The most constructive and spiritually praiseworthy response Humanistic Christians can make when abortion-related issues come into their consciousness is to do all that they can to make awareness of contraceptive options more widely known and socially acceptable to people who are sexually active, or planning to become so.

There is only one path to salvation, and being on it means believing in the truth of Christian dogma

If one wanted to capture the essence of the attitude of authoritarian leaders in any sphere in a single short sentence, 'My way is the only way' would be quite a good way of doing it. There is no room for alternatives to the rigid dogmas created by those of an authoritarian disposition who are powerful in any organisation. The Christian Church provides a perfect example of this sort of situation.

For those making up the authoritarian face of Christianity, the religion does not just offer an absolutely trustworthy 'path to salvation'. More than that, they generally believe it offers the **only** path to salvation from eternal punishment for all humanity's wrongdoing. No spiritual insights claimed to be possessed by any other religion are valid unless they are also to be found within Christianity.

From the perspective of Humanistic Christianity, the amount of anxiety generated in those whose Christianity is of the authoritarian type by any member of the Church who espouses ideas which contradict any of the propositions of orthodox Christian dogma would be amusing if the way in which that anxiety manifests itself did not have such serious consequences for the reputation of the religion as a whole, and for the peace and happiness of many people within it. Excommunication and/or the threat of it is one of the more vicious control mechanisms employed to try to safeguard uniformity of belief and practice by some branches of the Christian Church. Best known for the role it plays in the thinking of the Vatican-based Roman Catholic Church, it is, however, also one of the control mechanisms used by some fringe Protestant Churches against those who deviate from full acceptance of the dogmas of their particular version of 'the one true faith'.

The dogmatically held belief that, 'my way is the only way', is bad enough in terms of its effects on people's spiritual sensitivities – as A. N. Whitehead said in his *Religion in the Making*, 'Religions commit suicide when they find their inspirations in their dogmas', but the same arrogant assumption of superiority exhibited by many authoritarian Christians in their religious prejudices is at the root of the racial and cultural prejudice and homophobic and sometimes anti-Semitic attitudes which are very frequently encountered among authoritarian Christians. These prejudices are all ultimately traceable to deeply-rooted, mostly unconscious feelings of inferiority, against which the self-delusion of a self-congratulatory attitude of superiority is erected as a defence.

Unfortunately the defensive sense of superiority in religious matters, where it exists, makes religion very vulnerable to being drawn into disputes motivated by political and sometimes territorial issues, and sometimes being used as just a way of rationalising a hatred of oppressors generated by years of abuse. The 'civil war' in Ireland, ostensibly a Catholic/Protestant clash, had in fact got virtually nothing to do with religious differences between Roman Catholics and Protestants, religious differences between whom were to a very large extent just a convenient peg on which to hang justification for a primarily socio-political conflict.

This is even more the case where the recent violent uprising of the Islamic State (IS) is concerned. This is often viewed as an Islam vs the West conflict, and therefore for many people as a conflict between Islam and Christianity, despite the fact that, as Muslim leaders are increasingly strongly pointing out, the ideology of IS has got nothing to do with Islamic theology. In a not dissimilar way the Crusades, sold to generations of school children in the West in school history lessons as a heroic attempt to defend Christianity against its enemies was really nothing of the sort. It is doubtful whether any of those fighting for the 'defence of Christianity' in those conflicts had any significant understanding of what the religion they saw themselves as defending was all about, and the vast majority of them would have been almost totally ignorant of the religious views of their enemy. The Crusades were not primarily motivated by any religious fervour – it was territorial and socio-political factors that were the primary issues driving the enthusiasm of some Christians to undertake the Crusades.

Although all the blame for these and other so-called religious conflicts cannot be laid at the door of the noisily proclaimed belief of some Christians that their religion has a monopoly on religious truth, repeatedly beating that drum is not conducive to good relations with other religious groupings. And Christianity is at least as guilty as any other religion of being provocatively aggressive towards what are seen as competitors. Although the Crusades stand out as a strikingly high point of Christian-instigated violence towards Muslims, they were by no means an isolated phenomenon, and violence from some right-wing Christians towards Muslim religion is sadly still prevalent. Aggressive threats to publicly burn copies of the Koran by the leader of the singularly inappropriately named, and quite miniscule *Church of Dove World Outreach* in Florida in the United States in September 2010 was followed on March 20, 2011 by a 'Trial of the Quran' which was found to be guilty of 'crimes against humanity', following which the threatened public burning of a copy of that deeply venerated Muslim scripture took place. In the worldwide protests which erupted after that, many lives were lost. Any behaviour less worthy of being called Christian than that of Pastor Terry Jones in this matter is hard to imagine.

For Humanistic Christians, powerful insights into the nature of spiritual reality are of huge value wherever they are to be found, whether they are unique to their own religion, or to be found in religions other than Christianity or in other areas of study such as Psychology or Philosophy. That belief flows into a joyful embracing of the rich diversity of race, gender, sexual orientation, and the cultural and religious differences exhibited by the human race.

Chapter 5

So What is the Trouble with Christianity?

A system of dogmas may be the ark within which the Church floats safely down the flood-tide of history. But the Church will perish unless it opens its window and lets out the dove to search for an olive branch.

– Alfred North Whitehead. *Religion in the Making*

The name of Albert Einstein has gone down in history principally for the very important contribution he made to Theoretical Physics with his (at the time) revolutionary Theory of Relativity. But he not only made that and other highly significant contributions to Physics, he was also a profound thinker who, from time to time, expressed deeply thought-provoking ideas of a more philosophical nature.

Two of these are particularly relevant to the theme of this book. The one, which suggests that we need to look beneath the surface of material phenomena if we want an in-depth understanding of them is, 'There are two ways to live one's life. The one is as though nothing is a miracle. The other is as though everything is a miracle.'

The other, whose relevance to the ending of this book is perhaps more obvious, is, 'When the answer is simple, God is answering.' My answer to the questions, 'What is the trouble with Christianity – what is wrong with it?', and relatedly, 'When do we know that we are experiencing what a Humanistic Christian might want to describe as the 'presence of God'?' is simple, although of course not necessarily valuable because of its simplicity. But the fact that that answer is expressed in pretty straight-forward, non-technical, almost everyday language and meets the criterion for establishing whether or not one's intellectual endeavours have been worthwhile proposed by another great Theoretical Physicist, Erwin Schrödinger ('If you cannot – in the long run – tell everyone what you have been doing, your doing has been worthless'), will I hope recommend it to a wide variety of different readers.

Schrödinger's view in this matter echoes that of his fellow Theoretical Physicist Werner Heisenberg who said that, 'Even for the Physicist the description in plain language will be a criterion of the degree of understanding that has been reached', and both these opinions are entirely supported by another of Einstein's beliefs, that, 'Most of the fundamental ideas of science are essentially simple, and may, as a rule, be expressible in a language comprehensible to everyone.'

If those statements have any validity (and the impressive authority of the persons making them suggests that they should be taken very seriously), how much less necessary is it that theological speculations should inevitably be less easily understood than those of scientists about their particular area of specialisation. When a highly intelligent and spiritually sensitive person finds it impossible to see any truth in some aspect of standard Christian doctrine (such as the 'three-in-one and one-in-three' concept of the Trinity, or why an omnipotent God had no option but to have his 'dearly beloved son' subjected to torture and a horrible death) it is vanishingly unlikely that this is because of the limitations of human intelligence, (although that intelligence undoubtedly does have its limitations). To try to explain away any theological improbability by saying that with man some things are impossible, but with God everything is possible is just an intellectual cop-out. It is infinitely more likely that the reason why that person, and the many others like him or her cannot see the truth of these ideas, is simply that those ideas are wrong, probably illogical, and very possibly internally inconsistent.

In my experience, much of Christian Theology is fairly

impenetrable to those who have not been indoctrinated into the language, concepts, and frankly often weird theories about the nature of God and 'his' relationship with humanity. For me at least, the whole paraphernalia of theories about the existence of an omnipotent, omniscient, and omnipresent creator of the universe, heaven, and hell, and the virgin birth of his only son whose death he decreed as a necessary atonement for the otherwise unforgivable sins of the human race he once pronounced to be 'very good' (Genesis 1:31) has hardly ever had any connection with my experience of life. Sometimes when coming across some aspect of Christian Theology I had not encountered before, I am irresistibly reminded of Arthur Koestler's memorable description of the history of English Criminal Law as 'A wonderland, filled with the braying of learned asses'.[33]

And so, in drawing this book to a close, I give a brief statement of my simple answer to the question I set out to answer in writing it – 'What is the trouble with Christianity? What is wrong with it, and why has a system of thought which contains within itself such a powerful set of ethical principles not only made so relatively little contribution to making the world a better place for all living creatures, but to a most distressing extent, actually contributed to making it a worse one?' By way of amplifying that answer just a little, I look briefly at the further question of when, in my opinion, it is appropriate to think of ourselves as being in the presence of God – what real identifiable emotional reaction in that mind-body-spirit unity which is the human being, signals that that might be a helpful way of describing our experience.

What is wrong with Christianity?
Unfortunately, a great deal. Most seriously, I believe, because most far-reaching in its effects, is the widespread prevalence of authoritarian attitudes and behaviours in people in positions of

influence within the religion. This has led to a number of damaging consequences for Christianity:

1. For one thing the obsession with issues of control manifested by authoritarian religious people has seriously interfered with their ability to perceive some aspects of the concept of gentleness (which is such an important issue in the ethical principles taught by Jesus), and with their ability to accept the undesirability for human welfare of aggressive attempts to coercively control the thinking and behaviour of others. Associated with this is an attitude of dogmatic intolerance towards other religions – the belief that Christianity provides the one and only path to salvation.

2. The intolerant belief in the necessity for compulsion in attempts to modify people's behaviour and beliefs is both a result of, and a contribution to the widespread development within Christianity (and perhaps other religions), of a concept of God as a being external to, and in control of the universe, the ultimate authority figure for everyone in that universe. Authoritarian submission to the 'will' of this being is seen as the greatest religious virtue. Although in theory it is 'submission to the will of God' which Authoritarian Christianity promotes, it is in reality submissive acceptance of the beliefs of those powerful in leadership positions within the Church that Authoritarian Christianity demands of us.

3. To a dispassionate observer this being bears a remarkable similarity in many respects to the believer's parents – the first authority figures in most people's lives. Freud's assertion that, 'God is at bottom nothing but an exalted father'[34] has a great deal of truth in it so far as the concept of God embedded in Authoritarian Christianity is concerned. However that criticism does not apply at all to

the very different 'God as a property of the universe' concept of God which underlies Humanistic Christianity.

4. Among the many psychopathologies for which the obsession with authoritarian control has provided fertile soil in which to flourish, are two particularly unfortunate and untrue beliefs about human Psychology: one is that punishment is an unavoidable necessity if we are to ensure 'good behaviour' from people. The other is that human beings are fatally flawed, that they are fundamentally wicked, and 'incline towards sin'. These beliefs lie at the root of the denigration of the value of pleasure (especially sexual pleasure), and the sadistic and masochistic glorification of pain and suffering which is one of the very unattractive, and most damaging and destructive characteristics of Authoritarian Christianity.

5. For some authoritarianly-inclined Christians all humans are inherently wicked, but women are possessed of an extra dose of badness, and must be kept in their subordinate place by males who have a God-given duty to be the dominant partner in all male-female relationships. Women cannot be trusted. After all isn't it the fault of that arch-temptress Eve that humankind was booted out of paradise into a world of continual struggle in our attempts to find happiness?

6. Underlying all these pathologies is the belief that there is an endemically adversarial relationship between an all-good, controlling God and a chronically disobedient human race. This belief is probably the reason why much of the Christian Church sees its mission in life as to define what constitutes 'being good', and to try to intimidate people into being what the particular branch of the Church to which they belong regards as 'good'. The Christian Church could, to its great advantage, give some long overdue attention to William Blake, the nineteenth-century

English Christian mystic's penetratingly insightful refor-
mulation of the traditional Christian doctrine of 'Original
Sin' as not disobedience, but rather as the adversarial
attitude.

The humanistic tradition within the Christian Church rejects the
authoritarian concepts and autocratic behaviours manifest in
Authoritarian Christianity, and cherishes instead the importance
of influence rather than attempts to control the behaviour of
others. The way in which this approach seeks WIN-WIN resolu-
tions of conflict, based on the ethical principles underlying Jesus'
teaching, is well illustrated in a brief summary by Harold Loukes
of one of the reasons why the Quaker movement so whole-
heartedly embraces Jesus' belief that gentleness is ultimately
stronger than violence. He writes:

Seek not to crush tyrants but to awaken men's minds to the
loving spirit in which they will desire to put by the fruits of
tyranny. Counter falsehood with truth, ignorance with
knowledge, hardness of heart with a tenderness that seeks the
victims of wrong. So shall you save the victim from his tyrant
and the tyrant from his tyranny.

It is also beautifully illustrated in a very brief little poem by
Edwin Markham:

He drew a circle that shut me out. Heretic, rebel, a thing to
flout. But love and I had the wit to win: We drew a circle that
took him in.

Those thoughts flow directly from what we know of Jesus' beliefs
about the sorts of behaviours which belong in the Kingdom of
Heaven.

Ye have heard that it hath been said, Thou shalt love thy neighbour, and hate thine enemy. But I say unto you, Love your enemies, bless them that curse you, do good to them that hate you, and pray for them which despitefully use you, and persecute you; That ye may be the children of your Father which is in Heaven (Matthew 5:43-45).

An important aspect of the multifaceted trouble with Christianity is that, to judge from the way they behave, too few of the adherents of that religion believe in the truth and value of the ethical principles which Jesus urged upon us. With the rise of the Pentecostal movement, the 'born agains', and of a right-wing within Christianity, there seems to have recently been a groundswell within the religion of movement towards a narcissistic obsession with the question of personal salvation – salvation from an eternity of suffering at the hands of a God who exists only as a nightmarish fantasy of traumatised people. In the process, the ethical principles espoused by Jesus of Nazareth seem to no longer occupy a centre-stage position within Christianity. The more people who do identify with those ethical principles and act on them, the closer humanity will get to creating the Kingdom of Heaven here on earth, and come to know 'The peace of God which passeth all understanding'.

There are some hopeful signs of the weakening of the influence of authoritarian attitudes within at least the Roman Catholic branch of the Christian Church which has been racked by increasing protests within its ranks recently. The breakaway movement of the Old Catholic Church, which among other things ordains women priests and does not accept the doctrine of Papal Infallibility was an early (mid-nineteenth century) example of the refusal by a significant number of committed members of the Catholic Church to continue to bow to autocratic Vatican control. More recently, the establishment of the Austrian Priests' Initiative, and the increasingly widespread ignoring of the

Church's prohibition of the use of contraception by sexually active members of the Catholic laity are just two of the more high profile rebellions against authoritarian Vatican control of all aspects of the lives of Catholics.

The Austrian Priests' Initiative is a most interesting pioneering example of what may well become a significant development within the Catholic Church. It consists of a group of more than 300 priests, under the leadership of a former Vicar-General of Vienna, Mgr Helmut Schüller, which has formed an organisation openly calling for disobedience to the dictates of the Vatican-based Church in respect of priestly celibacy and Holy Communion for remarried divorcees and non-Catholics. It also supports women priests, lay preachers, and the use of the term 'Priestless Eucharists'. The organisation also seems to support homosexual unions. Public support for the actions of the Priests' Initiative has been estimated to be over seventy per cent, with a similar percentage of Austria's 3500 Catholic priests approving of at least parts of their programme.

Even more likely to eventually completely undermine the overpowering influence of authoritarian attitudes in the at present all-male, and often misogynistic power hierarchy within the Vatican-based Roman Catholic Church, is the arrival of another rebellious organisation within its ranks – Roman Catholic Womenpriests. Relatively few people as yet (in 2015) seem to know about the existence of this movement, but it has a feeling about it of an idea whose time has come. On the Danube River in 2002 seven women were secretly ordained by two (male[35]) Roman Catholic Bishops, and now, 13 years later, there are nearly 200 Catholic women worldwide functioning as ordained priests with full sacramental and preaching authority, all of them dedicated Christians and committed to their Catholic identity, and all of them automatically excommunicated by the Vatican for defying their Church's Canon Law, item number 1024.

It remains to be seen how the recent arrival of the reforming

Pope Francis in the Vatican will play out, but so far it looks as though his attitudes and behaviours will also weaken to at least some extent the authoritarian attitudes which have prevailed so strongly in that branch of Christianity. The impressively rapid growth of a culture of dissent from autocratically imposed rigidities is hopefully just one more sign that, using the symbolism of Christopher Fry's poem *The Sleep of Prisoners* with which I started this book,

> The frozen misery
> Of centuries breaks, cracks, begins to move;
> The thunder is the thunder of the floes ...

The thunder is indeed the thunder of the break up of frozen thoughts and attitudes, and as the poem goes on to claim, the enterprise is indeed 'exploration into God'. The purging from that concept of those psychopathological components which have made 'the fear of God' such a frightening and depressing reality to so many people, and left them vulnerable to emotionally manipulative attempts to sign them up for authoritarian submission to the dictates of autocratic religious leaders is a fundamentally important task for those seeking to transform the trouble within Christianity to joy. Some emotionally mature religious leaders are doing wonderful work of compassionate love in the world and in their churches, but unfortunately there are many more who may mean well, but because of their authoritarian mindset, are doing a great deal of harm to the psychological and spiritual development of their followers.

How do we know when we are in the presence of what a Humanistic Christian would describe as God?
A personal, Not-the-Nicene Creed

I find it appropriate and helpful to label as 'an awareness of the presence of God' the emotional experience I have when I behave, and/or see others behaving in ways which are consistent with the ethical principles urged upon us 2000 years ago by Jesus of Nazareth – specifically when:

We feel a compassionate concern for the physical and/or psychological suffering of people and animals, and do what we can to minimise their pain, heal their hurt, and lift from them at least some of the burdens they are carrying.

Our attitude to the people we are interacting with is more one of, 'How can I enhance the quality of this person's life?' than it is of, 'What can I get out of this person?'

We treat all people, and very especially children, with respect in regard to their unique personalities, helping them to become more fully themselves, and to be authentic in their presentation of themselves to the world.

We have a choice between being right and being kind, and we choose to be kind.

Our behaviour reflects our belief that gentleness is ultimately stronger than violence.

We remember the Power of the Positive, the fact that whilst it is true that 'punishment can sometimes do much, encouragement can always do more', and that in the words of another old proverb, 'More people are flattered into virtue than are bullied out of vice', and when our behaviour reflects our belief in those truths.

We treat anyone (including ourselves) who in our eyes has done something wrong, with kind, compassionate forgiveness, and leave them with some thoughts and feelings which will bring them a degree of peace and comfort in their distress, and will help them to avoid similar wrongdoing in the future.

We feel concern for the mental mess, the baggage left by previous traumatic experiences that sometimes drives people to hurt others, and we remember Jesus' response to those who wanted to stone to death the woman caught in the act of adultery, 'Let he who is without sin cast the first stone.'

We look after our minds and bodies in such a way that we have the strength, the stamina, the resources and the motivation to live a happy and fulfilling life, and to do what we can to make the lives of all living creatures as happy and fulfilling as our own.

We spend time contemplating beauty – in nature, in any form of art, in music, literature, painting, sculpture, or in mathematics or any other field of human endeavour.

> **Whenever we do any of these things, we are manifesting the presence of God within us, and leave the world with a stronger impress of God upon it.**

For the Humanistic Christian, only some such conception of the nature of God as that embedded in the above is appropriate to lie at the heart of Christianity. Such a concept was hinted at by Albert Schweitzer when he said, 'The relationship between the Will to Live, the Will to Love, and God is the most profound problem to which Philosophy can address itself.' The more progress we can make in that sort of understanding of the Nature of God, the closer we shall be able to get to making the Unitarian Hymn-writer Marion Franklin Ham's vision of the future

Christian Church a present reality:

As tranquil streams that meet and merge
And flow as one to seek the sea,
Our kindred hearts and minds unite
To build a church that shall be free.

A freedom that reveres the past,
But trusts the dawning future more,
And bids the soul, in search of truth,
Adventure boldly and explore.

Free from the bonds that bind the mind
To narrow thought and lifeless creed,
Free from a social code that fails
To serve the cause of human need.

Prophetic church, the future waits
Your liberating ministry,
Go forward in the power of love,
Proclaim the truth that makes us free.
  – *Marion Franklin Ham* (1867-1956)

Appendix

Progress in truth – truth of science and truth of religion – is mainly a progress in the framing of concepts, in discarding artificial abstractions or partial metaphors, and in evolving notions which strike more deeply into the root of reality. For it is not true that there is easy apprehension of the great formative generalities. They are embedded under the rubbish of irrelevant detail. The great intuitions, which in their respective provinces set all things right, dawn but slowly upon history.
– Alfred North Whitehead. *Religion in the Making*

I end this book with a number of quotations from various (all but two non-biblical) sources, which when I come across them never fail to deepen my own spiritual experience. I believe that we can abstract from them some of the intellectual ideas which together form the conceptual infrastructure of a Humanistic Christian's Concept of God. It is my hope that readers will find that slowly and reflectively reading through these quotes heightens whatever enthusiasm they already have for the ethical principles embedded in Humanistic Christianity.

From Kahlil Gibran's *The Prophet*:

The teacher who walks in the shadow of the temple, among his followers, gives not of his wisdom, but rather of his faith and his lovingness. If he is indeed wise he does not bid you enter the house of his wisdom, but rather leads you to the threshold of your own mind.

It is the mark of an educated mind, to entertain a thought without accepting it.
– Aristotle

From one of a series of thought-provoking little cameos constructed by the liberal Roman Catholic priest, Father Anthony de Mello:

To the disciple who was overly respectful the Master said, "Light is reflected on a wall. Why venerate the wall? Be attentive to the light."

The highest thought is ineffable. It must be felt from one person to another, but cannot be articulated – our profoundest and most important convictions are unspeakable.
 – Samuel Butler

The heart has reasons that reason cannot know.
 – Blaise Pascal

And another thought from Blaise Pascal:

It has pleased God that divine verities should not enter the heart through the understanding, but the understanding through the heart.

From the writings of Ralph Waldo Emerson:

Within man is the soul of the whole; the wise silence; the universal beauty, to which every part and particle is equally related; the eternal One. When it breaks through his intellect, it is genius; when it breathes through his will, it is virtue; when it flows through his affections, it is love.

From an old Latin hymn:

'Ubi caritas et amor, Deus ibi est', which is translated as: 'Where charity and love are, there is God.'

In the end, it won't matter how much you have, but rather how much you have given. It won't matter how much you know, but rather how much you love. And it won't matter how much you profess to believe, but rather how deeply you live the few enduring truths you claim as ultimate.

– Anon

From the autobiography of Albert Schweitzer:

As one who tries to remain youthful in his thinking and feeling, I have struggled against facts and experience on behalf of belief in the good and the true. At the present time when violence, clothed in life, dominates the world more cruelly than it ever has before, I still remain convinced that truth, love, peaceableness, meekness, and kindness are the power that can master all violence. The world will be theirs as soon as ever a sufficient number of men and women with purity of heart, with strength, and with perseverance think and live out the thoughts of love and truth, of meekness and peaceableness.

All violence produces its own limitations, for it calls forth an answering violence which sooner or later becomes its equal or its superior. But kindness works simply and perseveringly; it produces no strained relations which prejudice its working; strained relations which already exist it relaxes. Mistrust and misunderstanding it puts to flight, and it strengthens itself by calling forth answering kindness. Hence it is the furthest-reaching and the most effective of all forces.

From the autobiography, *The Unquiet Mind,* of Kay Redfield Jamieson, a Psychiatrist who suffers from Bipolar disorder:

We all build internal sea walls to keep at bay the sadnesses of life and the often overwhelming forces within our minds. In whatever way we do this – through love, work, family, faith, friends, denial, alcohol, drugs or medication – we build these walls, stone by stone, over a lifetime. One of the most difficult problems is to construct these barriers of such a height and strength that one has a true harbour, a sanctuary away from crippling turmoil and pain, but yet low enough and permeable enough, to let in fresh seawater that will fend off the inevitable inclination toward brackishness.

Let us be kind to one another for most of us are fighting a hard battle.
– Ian McLaren

A poem by Stevie Smith entitled, *Not Waving, but Drowning*:

Nobody heard him, the dead man,
But still he lay moaning:
I was much further out than you thought
And not waving but drowning.

Poor chap, he always loved larking
And now he's dead
It must have been too cold for him his heart gave way,
They said.

Oh, no no no, it was too cold always
(Still the dead one lay moaning)
I was much too far out all my life
And not waving, but drowning.

The ideals which have lighted my way, and time after time have given me new courage to face life cheerfully, have been Kindness, Beauty, and Truth.
– Albert Einstein

It is the history of our kindnesses that alone makes this world tolerable ... If it were not for that, for the effect of kind words, kind looks, kind letters ... I should be inclined to think our life a practical jest in the worst possible spirit.
– Robert Louis Stevenson

It is a little embarrassing that, after forty-five years of research and study, the best advice that I can give to people is to be a little kinder to each other.
– Aldous Huxley

From one of the autobiographical writings (entitled *Why I Am Not A Christian*) of the influential twentieth-century atheistic philosopher, Bertrand Russell:

There are certain things that our age needs, and certain things it should avoid. It needs compassion, and a desire that mankind be happy: it needs the desire for knowledge and the determination to eschew pleasant myths; it needs above all courageous hope and the impulse to creativeness. ... The root of the matter is a very simple and old-fashioned thing, a thing so simple that I am almost ashamed to mention it for fear of the derisive smile with which wise cynics will greet my words. The thing I mean – please forgive me for mentioning it – is love, Christian love, or compassion. If you feel this, you have a motive for existence, a guide in action, a reason for courage, an imperative necessity for intellectual honesty.

An anonymous summary of the essence of Christian ethics:

If it comes to a choice between being right or being kind, choose kind.

There were rules in the monastery, but the Master always

warned against the tyranny of the law. "Obedience keeps the rules," he would say, "Love knows when to break them".
– Father Anthony de Mello.

From Victor Hugo:

You can give without loving, but you can never love without giving. The great acts of love are done by those who are habitually performing small acts of kindness. We pardon to the extent that we love. Love is knowing that even when you are alone, you will never be lonely again, and great happiness of life is the conviction that we are loved, loved for ourselves, and even loved in spite of ourselves.

If I ... understand all mysteries and all knowledge, and if I have all faith, so as to remove mountains, but do not have love, I am nothing. ... Love is patient; love is kind; love is not envious or boastful or arrogant or rude. It does not insist on its own way; it is not irritable or resentful; it does not rejoice in wrongdoing, but rejoices in the truth. It bears all things, believes all things, hopes all things, endures all things. Love never ends. ... And now faith, hope, and love abide; and the greatest of these is love.
– St Paul

Love is a flower, and you its only seed.
– Anon

The fruit of the Spirit is love, joy, peace, longsuffering, gentleness goodness, faith, meekness, (and) temperance.
– St Paul

The ripeness that our development must aim at is one which makes us simpler, more truthful, purer, more peace-loving,

meeker, kinder, more sympathetic. That is the only way we are to sober down with age. That is the process in which the soft iron of youthful idealism hardens into the steel of a full-grown idealism which can never be lost. ... The knowledge of life, therefore which we grown-ups have to pass on to the younger generation will not be expressed thus: 'Reality will soon give way before your ideals, but 'Grow into your ideals, so that life can never rob you of them'. ... If all of us could become what we were at fourteen what a different place the world would be!
– Albert Schweitzer

All things work together for good to those whose heart is in the right place.
– An anonymous rewording of an idea expressed originally by St Paul

The great aim of education is not knowledge, but action.
– Herbert Spencer

To be satisfied with your possessions, but not contented with yourself until you have made the best of them; ... to be governed by your admirations rather than your disgusts; to covet nothing that is your neighbour's except his kindness of heart and gentleness of manners; ...These are little guide-posts on the footpath to peace.
– Henry van Dyke

Where there is hate, let me sow love,
Where there is wrong, forgiveness,
Where there is discord, harmony,
Where there is error, truth,
Where there is doubt, belief,
Where there is despair, hope,

Where there is darkness, light,
Where there is sorrow, joy.
Let me strive more to comfort others
Than to be comforted,
To understand others than to be understood,
To love others more than to be loved.
For it is in giving that we receive;
It is in forgiving others that we ourselves are forgiven.
– A prayer attributed to St. Francis of Assisi

It is one of the most beautiful compensations of this life that no man can sincerely try to help another without helping himself. ... Serve and thus you shall be served.
– Ralph Waldo Emerson

Example is not the main thing in influencing others. It is the only thing.
– Albert Schweitzer

You cannot shake hands with a clenched fist.
– Indira Gandhi

Who you are shouts so loudly in my ears that I cannot hear what you are saying.
– Ralph Waldo Emerson

One day a man was walking along a beach littered with thousands of starfish washed up after a storm and gradually dying from lack of contact with their natural environment – the sea. After a time he came upon a young woman repeatedly bending down to pick up a starfish and then throwing it as far as she could back into the sea. Intrigued by what the woman was doing he stopped and asked her why she was tackling such an outfacingly huge task. "There are

thousands of these creatures dying on this beach", he said. "You won't make any significant difference with the few you are able to save." Picking up another one she threw it back into the sea and said, "Well it made a difference to that one."
– Anon

There is an old Hasidic story of the Rabbi who had a conversation with the Lord about Heaven and Hell. "I will show you Hell," said the Lord and led the Rabbi into a room in the middle of which was a very big, round table. The people sitting at it were famished and desperate. In the middle of the table there was a large pot of stew, enough and more for everyone. The smell of the stew was delicious and made the Rabbi's mouth water. The people round the table were holding spoons with very long handles. Each one found that it was just possible to reach the pot to take a spoonful of the stew, but because the handle of his spoon was longer than a man's arm, he could not get the food back into his mouth. The Rabbi saw that their suffering was terrible. "Now I will show you Heaven," said the Lord, and they went into another room, exactly the same as the first. There was the same big, round table and the same pot of stew. The people, as before, were equipped with the same long-handled spoons – but here they were well nourished and plump, laughing and talking. At first the Rabbi could not understand. "It is simple, but it requires a certain skill," said the Lord. "You see, they have learned to feed each other."
– Irwin Yalom

God Appears & God is Light
To those poor Souls who dwell in Night,
But does a Human Form Display
To those who Dwell in Realms of day.
– William Blake

I sought my soul
But my soul I could not see.
I sought my God
But my God eluded me.
I sought my brother
And I found all three.
– Anon

One of William Blake's *Songs of Innocence* entitled *The Divine Image*:

To Mercy, Pity, Peace, and Love
All pray in their distress;
And to these virtues of delight
Return their thankfulness.

For Mercy, Pity, Peace, and Love
Is God, our father dear,
And Mercy, Pity, Peace, and Love
Is man, his child and care.

For Mercy has a human heart,
Pity a human face,
And Love, the human form divine,
And Peace, the human dress.

Then every man, of every clime,
That prays in his distress,
Prays to the human form divine,
Love, Mercy, Pity, Peace.

And all must love the human form,
In heathen, turk or Jew;
Where Mercy, Love, and Pity dwell
There God is dwelling too.

We never move toward the divine by ignoring the human.
– William Lynch

To give pleasure to a single heart by a single act is better than
a thousand heads bowing in prayer.
– Mahatma Gandhi

Anyone can be polite to a king; it takes a great man or woman
to be polite to a beggar.
– Anon

A grocer came to the Master in great distress to say that across
the way from his shop they had opened a large chain store
that would drive him out of business. His family had owned
his shop for a century, and to lose it now would be his
undoing, for there was nothing else he was skilled at.

Said the Master, "If you fear the owner of the chain store,
you will hate him. And hatred will be your undoing."

"What shall I do?" said the distraught grocer.

"Each morning walk out of your shop onto the sidewalk
and bless your shop, wishing it prosperity. Then turn to face
the chain store and bless it too."

"What? Bless my competitor and destroyer?"

"Any blessing you give him will rebound to your good.
Any evil you wish him will destroy you."

After six months the grocer returned to report that he had
had to close down his shop as he had feared, but he was now
in charge of the chain store and his affairs were in better shape
than ever before.
– Father Anthony de Mello

In the course of my studies, I have discovered that the
religious quest is not about discovering 'the truth' or 'the
meaning of life', but about living as intensely as possible here

and now. The idea is not to latch onto some superhuman personality or to 'get to heaven' but to discover how to be fully human.
– Karen Armstrong

But the churchmen fain would kill their church, as the churches have killed their Christ.
– Alfred Lord Tennyson

From the seventeenth-century English poet, John Dryden:

By education most have been misled;
So they believe because they were so bred,
The priest continues what the nurse began,
And thus the child imposes on the man.

An elderly Sioux Indian Chief was telling his story to an Indian boy.

He said: "I have two wolves fighting in my heart. One wolf represents happiness, joy, forgiving, love, respect, sympathy, empathy, generosity and compassion. The other wolf represents hatred, misery, anger, contempt, insolence, intolerance, selfishness, violence and greed."

The boy asked, "Which wolf will win?"

The wise old Chief replied, "The one I feed".
– Anon

There is an as yet unmeasured depth of meaning in that strange saying of Jesus that, "Blessed are the meek, for they shall inherit the earth".
– Albert Schweitzer

Also from Albert Schweitzer:

A man is truly ethical only when he obeys the compulsion to help all life which he is able to assist, and shrinks from injuring anything that lives. ... If he walks on the road after a shower and sees an earthworm which has strayed onto it, he bethinks himself that it must get dried up in the sun if it does not return soon enough to ground into which it can burrow, so he lifts it from the deadly stone surface, and puts it on the grass. If he comes across an insect which has fallen into a puddle, he stops a moment in order to hold out a leaf or a stalk on which it can save itself.

We are all like ice-blocks slowly melting into the most unbelievably warm and welcoming ocean of eternal Love and Light ... as we slowly melt absolutely nothing will be lost; all will be perfectly absorbed into the oneness of the All ... a unity of Love beyond our wildest imaginings!

– Anon

Notes

1. There is a rather lovely (4:24 minute) video based on this poem at http://bit.ly/sleep-of-prisoners.

2. Most of this 'technical detail' comes from the field of Neuropsychology – the specialised branch of Psychology which takes very seriously the fact that 'mind' and 'body' are two aspects of one underlying human reality. Our mental states of thought and feeling do not *just* float around in some isolated world of non-physical unreality, but are all associated with some physical state in our bodies. A very important part of that physical component of all our psychological experience lies in the activity of our nervous system, that incredibly complex network of brain, spinal cord, and peripheral and autonomic nerves, parts of which innervate every area of the human body.

3. Published towards the end of 2014 by John Hunt Publishers, London under their *Christian Alternative* imprint.

4. Even more shocking than some of what is contained in a pamphlet put out recently by Islamic State (IS) in which the view is expressed that, 'It is permissible to buy, sell, or give as a gift female captives and slaves, for they are merely property, which can be disposed of.'

5. Geza Vermes. *Christian Beginnings: From Nazareth to Nicaea, AD 30-325*, London: Allen Lane, 2012, p. 135.

6. CE = 'Of the Common Era' and BCE = 'Before the Common Era', are the terms modern scholars prefer to use rather than the better-known 'BC' (= 'Before Christ') and AD (= 'Anno Domini' = the Latin for 'in the year of the Lord').

7. The mathematical processes of addition, subtraction, multiplication and division are perhaps the best-known examples of non-physical realities.

8. A. N. Whitehead. *The Concept of Nature*, Cambridge:

Cambridge University Press, 1920.

9. As the theoretical physicist Erwin Schrödinger put it, 'The observing mind is not a physical system; it cannot interact with any physical system.'

10. Kolb & Whishaw: *Fundamentals of Human Neuropsychology* (2003) is a useful source of information summarising what we know about the human senses.

11. All the biblical quotations used in this book come from either the original 1611 King James Version of the English Bible or the New Revised Standard Version, the more modern translation favoured by most biblical scholars today, or some combination of the two.

12. Albert Schweitzer. *Civilization and Ethics*, London: Adam and Charles Black, 1923, p. 243.

13. Ibid p. 242.

14. Ibid p.243-4.

15. Quoted in George Seaver. *Albert Schweitzer: The Man and his Mind,* London: Adam and Charles Black, 1955, p. 309.

16. Joseph Fletcher. *Situational Ethics: The New Morality*, London: SCM Press, 1966.

17. A. N. Whitehead. *Modes of Thought,* Cambridge: Cambridge University Press, 1938.

18. Joseph Fletcher. *Situational Ethics: The New Morality*, London: SCM Press, 1966, p. 13.

19. Ibid, p. 20.

20. Each one of us has our own idea about what it means to live 'a successful life'. Ralph Waldo Emerson whose writings have provided so many memorable quotes had a definition of success which powerfully expresses a view which is absolutely consistent with the ethics of humanitarian Christianity. 'To laugh often and to love much; to win the respect of intelligent persons and the affection of children; to earn the approbation of honest critics and endure the betrayal of false friends; to appreciate beauty; to find the best

in others; to give oneself; to leave the world a bit better whether by a healthy child, a garden patch or a redeemed social condition; to have played and laughed with enthusiasm and sung with exultation; to know even one life has breathed easier because you have lived: this is to have succeeded.'

21. Melanie Parry (Ed). *Chambers Biographical Dictionary*, Edinburgh: Larousse, 1997.

22. What does seem to have had more impact on that institution are his truly appalling ideas about the nature of women. Women are 'misbegotten or deformed males' – a woman results when something goes wrong at conception. Thomas Aquinas (1225-1274) deriving his views on women from Aristotle and Augustine, believed that the entire nature of woman was inferior: in body (weaker), in mind (less capable of reason), and morally (less capable of will and moral self-control), and this inferiority had been deepened by sin. He concluded that God only created woman because of her role in procreation. Of course Aquinas was a child of his time and thought and wrote as part of a long tradition of misogyny in Judeo-Christian religion, one of the earliest examples of which is to be seen in the biblical Book of Genesis where it is proclaimed (Genesis 3:16) that men shall rule over women. This 'proclamation' is just one example among many, of anxious and insecure males projecting their sexual problems onto God, which continues within Christianity at least, right down to the present day.

I am grateful to Mary Ryan, one of the small band of fully ordained female Roman Catholic priests, for bringing to my attention the issue of Aquinas's attitudes towards female sexuality. The continuing presence of attitudes of this type in the thinking of the majority of those powerful in the Vatican hierarchy is doubtless what lies behind their recent extraordinary decision to raise the 'sin' of even discussing the issue of ordaining women priests to the level of 'highest crime' (DELICTA GRAVIORA). In doing this the Vatican is equating the sinfulness of disobedience in this matter with that of paedophilia. The mind boggles. From the perspective of Humanistic Christianity the Vatican has completely lost its way in this matter. Mary Ryan's very moving book, *Loving Fiercely: Women, violence, and a God who cares* is a fascinating source of information about this potentially powerful organisation-changing development within the Roman Catholic Church.

23. According to the Concise Oxford English Dictionary a metaphor is 'a figure of speech in which a word or phrase is applied to something to which it is not literally applicable, a thing regarded as symbolic of something else'.

24. Anthropomorphic ideas about the nature of God have indeed been around in Judeo-Christian religion for a long time. One of the most ludicrous examples of this is to be found in a book written somewhere in the period of the seventh to the tenth centuries CE called Shi'ur Koma (Estimation of the height), in which God is described as a huge being in human shape. The measurement of his various body parts, eyes, ears, lips, neck, beard, ankles, etc. is given in parasangs. The Shorter Oxford English Dictionary defines a parasang as 'a Persian measure of length, usually reckoned as between 3 and 3½ English miles', but the writer of Shi'ur Koma hastens to inform us that the measurements he gives for God's body parts are not in earthly but rather in heavenly parasangs, each of which 'measures a million cubits, each cubit four spans, and each span reaches from one end of the world to the other'. Aaron Emmanuel Suffrin in James Hastings (Ed). *Encyclopaedia of Religion and Ethics,* Edinburgh: T. and T. Clark, 1913.

25. In a (copyrighted!) lecture entitled *The Beginning of Time,* to be found at

www.hawking.org.uk/the-beginning-of-time-html.

26. Ludovic Kennedy. *All in the mind – a farewell to God*, London: Hodder and Stoughton, 1999, p. 261.

27. As Emerson said in his *Uncollected Lectures. Natural Religion*, 'Other world! There is no other world! Here or nowhere is the whole fact.' The concept of Panentheism captures the basis of this idea well – 'God is immanent in nature, but transcendent of it'.

28. Those Christians who identify themselves as belonging in the Humanistic branch of that religion do not attend church services 'to worship God' or to hear from the 'religious experts' how 'He' wants them to live their lives. They go in order to increase their sensitivity to the spiritual depths of life – to become aware with renewed clarity of the power of goodness, beauty, and truth to promote human happiness and well-being. Christian church services differ widely in their ability to do this. For some of us the 1612 Anglican Prayer Book service of Evensong, when brought to life with timelessly beautiful music and in a beautiful architectural environment, provides a peak experience of that profoundly health- and happiness-enhancing state of knowing 'the peace of God that passeth all understanding'.

29. Alexander Solzhenitsyn, born in Russia in 1918 spent many years in prison under the Soviet regime.

30. 'Those who spare the rod hate their children, but those who love them are diligent to discipline them.' (Proverbs 13:24), and 'A wise child loves discipline' (Proverbs 13:1).

31. Forgiveness for our wrongdoing is something we all seek throughout our lives and never more desperately than when we are very young. Dag Hammarskjöld, that widely respected early Director-General of the United Nations expressed this thought beautifully when he wrote in his spiritual diary, 'Forgiveness is the answer to the child's dream of a miracle by which what is broken is made whole

again, what is soiled is again made clean,' and went on to expand this thought when he wrote, 'The dream explains why we need to be forgiven and why we must forgive. In the presence of God, nothing stands between Him and us – we *are* forgiven. But we *cannot* feel his presence if anything is allowed to stand between others and ourselves.' – Dag Hammarskjöld in *Markings*, London: Faber & Faber, 1964.

32. Bernárd Lynch. *If It Wasn't Love: Sex, Death and God*, Winchester: Circle Books, 2012, p.52.

33. Arthur Koestler. *Hanged by the Neck*, Harmondsworth, Penguin Books, 1961.

34. Sigmund Freud. *The Future of an Illusion*, London: Hogarth Press, 1927.

35. As all Roman Catholic Bishops at that time were. The Roman Catholic Womenpriests organisation now includes several female Bishops who for the most part now officiate at the ordination of new priestly recruits to the movement.

Bibliography

Karen Armstrong. *The Spiral Staircase,* New York: Harper Collins, 2004.

John de Gruchy. *Being Human: Confessions of a Christian Humanist,* London: SCM Press, 2006.

Ralph Waldo Emerson. *Uncollected Lectures. Natural Religion,* New York: W. E. Rudge, 1932.

Joseph Fletcher. *Situational Ethics: The New Morality,* London: SCM Press, 1966.

Matthew Fox. *Original Blessing: A Primer in Creation Spirituality,* Rochester, Vermont: Bear & Company, revised edition, 1996.

Erich Fromm. *Psychoanalysis and Religion,* New York: Bantam Books, 1950.

Kahlil Gibran. *The Prophet,* London: Heinemann, 1926.

Dag Hammarskjöld. *Markings,* London: Faber & Faber, 1964.

Kay Redfield Jamieson. *The Unquiet Mind,* London: Picador, 1997.

Ludovic Kennedy. *All in the mind – a farewell to God,* London: Hodder and Stoughton, 1999.

Arthur Koestler. *Hanged by the Neck,* Harmondsworth: Penguin Books, 1961.

Kolb & Whishaw: *Fundamentals of Human Neuropsychology,* Worth Publishers, 2003.

Harold Loukes. *The Quaker Contribution,* London: SCM Press, 1965.

Bernárd Lynch. *If It Wasn't Love: Sex, Death and God,* Winchester: Circle Books, 2012.

Philip Newell. *Christ of the Celts: The Healing of Creation,* Jossey-Bass, 2008.

Richard Oxtoby. *The Two Faces of Christianity,* London: John Hunt Publishers, 2014.

Richard Rohr. *Meditation on Original Blessing,* Wednesday July 8, 2015, https://cac.org.

Mary Ryan. *Loving fiercely: Women, Violence, and a God Who Cares,* Cape Town, 2014.

Albert Schweitzer. *Civilization and Ethics,* London: Adam and Charles Black, 1923.

Albert Schweitzer. *My Childhood and Youth,* London: Unwin Books, 1960.

Geza Vermes. *Christian Beginnings: From Nazareth to Nicaea, AD 30-325,* London: Allen Lane, 2012.

Alfred North Whitehead. *The Concept of Nature,* Cambridge: Cambridge University Press, 1920.

Alfred North Whitehead. *Science and the Modern World,* Cambridge: Cambridge University Press, 1925.

Alfred North Whitehead. *Religion in the Making,* Cambridge: Cambridge University Press, 1926.

Alfred North Whitehead. *Modes of Thought,* Cambridge: Cambridge University Press, 1938.

Additional Reading

Karen Armstrong. *Twelve Steps to a Compassionate Life*, London: The Bodley Head, 2011.

Cynthia Bourgeault. *The Meaning of Mary Magdalene: Discovering the Woman at the Heart of Christianity*, Boston: Shambhala, 2010.

Meg Chignell. *John on Jesus*, York, England, Sessions Book Trust, 1994.

Richard Dawkins. *The God Delusion*, London: Bantam Press, 2006.

Alain de Botton. *Religion for Atheists*, London, Penguin Books, 2012.

Trevor Greenfield. *An Introduction to Radical Theology*, Winchester, UK: O Books, 2006.

John Humphrys and Sarah Jarvis. *The Welcome Visitor*, London: Hodder and Stoughton, 2010.

Diarmaid MacCulloch. *The History of Christianity: The First Three Thousand Years*, London: Allen Lane, 2009, p. 218.

Daniel Maguire. *Christianity without God*, Gig Harbor, USA: Progressivechristianity, 2015.

Robin Meyers. *Saving Jesus from the Church*, New York: HarperCollins, 2009.

Brian Mountford. *Christian Atheist: Belonging without Believing*, Winchester: Circle Books, 2011.

Philip Newell. *Listening for the Heartbeat of God: A Celtic Spirituality*, Paulist Press, 1997.

Richard Oxtoby. *Achieving Our Full Potential: Towards More Effective Living*, Cape Town: New Voices, 2009.

Elaine Pagels. *The Gnostic Gospels*, London: Penguin, 1979.

John Robinson. *Honest to God*, London: SCM Press, 1963.

George Seaver. *Albert Schweitzer: The Man and his Mind*, London: Adam and Charles Black, 1955.

Bernard Spong. *Rescuing the Bible from Fundamentalism*, New

York: HarperCollins, 1991.

Bernard Spong. *Jesus for the Non-Religious*, New York: HarperCollins, 2007.

Geza Vermes. *The Authentic Gospel of Jesus,* London: Penguin Books, 2004.

Geza Vermes. *The Nativity: History and Legend,* London: Penguin, 2006.

A Few Words of Thanks

There is nothing like trying to write a book for reminding one that, as John Donne asserted, 'No man is an island, entire of itself'. If it were not for the network of interested and helpful people I am fortunate to be surrounded by, who have been generous in their encouragement of my writing of this book, and of at least some of its content, I might never have got it finished. My wife Colleen, and now-adult children Chris, Oliver, and Sven have been a constant source of help, support, and encouragement. I am particularly grateful to my son Dr Oliver Oxtoby for much editorial help and many fruitful discussions of the ideas in this book and its predecessor, *The Two Faces of Christianity*.

A number of friends and colleagues have been generous with the sharing of their insights and the interest (and sometimes excitement) they have shown in the development of those of my ideas which are expressed in this book. Corinna Arndt, Martin Brink, Rev. Peter Fox, Valda Führ, Anton Geldenhuys, Dr Despina Learmonth, Jenny McNulty, Rev. Gordon Oliver, Rev. Mary Ryan, Adam Struben, Rev. Harry Wiggett, Anja Wilkinson-Bienmüller, Dale Williams, and Margaret Young have all made contributions for which I am most grateful. I owe a particular debt of gratitude to my research assistants Louise-Mary Alexander, Marcelle Boshoff, Candice Edmunds, and Karla Hugo, who provided such skilled and cheerful help in getting the whole *The Two Faces of Christianity* and *The Trouble with Christianity* project going, and eventually brought to finality.

I am very conscious of the very significant part five people no longer physically living have played in shaping my thinking, and indeed my whole being: my warmly loving and constantly encouraging parents, Albert Schweitzer whose writings first aroused a passionate interest in the subject of Christian Ethics in me, the late Geza Vermes, Emeritus Professor of Jewish Studies at Oxford whom I was able to meet and learn much from a little while before his untimely death, and the person whom I never met but has been the greatest influence on my intellectual development, the Cambridge mathematician and profound Harvard philosopher Alfred North Whitehead. They all remain, in some sense, a timeless presence within me.

Also very importantly I must thank my publisher, John Hunt, London for establishing the *Christian Alternative* imprint as a home for books like this one, and for seeing a place for both *The Two Faces of Christianity* and *The Trouble with Christianity* in their list. Thank you John Hunt, Trevor Greenfield and my editor Denise Smith.

Finally, I am always happy to receive feedback, positive or negative, from readers, for which purpose my e-mail address is ro@richardoxtoby.co.za. In particular I would be glad to hear the opinions of readers as to what feelings within us constitute being aware of being in the presence of God, with my own current understanding of which I end Chapter 5.

Also by Richard Oxtoby

The Authoritarian Corruption of Christianity
The Two Faces of Christianity: A Psychological Analysis
Achieving Our Full Potential: Towards More Effective Living
*Releasing the Energy of the Organisation: Engaging Body, Mind, and
     Spirit in the World of Work*
Deep Structure Executive Coaching

CHRISTIAN
ALTERNATIVE

Throughout the two thousand years of Christian tradition there have been, and still are, groups and individuals that exist in the margins and upon the edge of faith. But in Christianity's contrapuntal history it has often been these outcasts and pioneers that have forged contemporary orthodoxy out of former radicalism as belief evolves to engage with and encompass the ever-changing social and scientific realities. Real faith lies not in the comfortable certainties of the Orthodox, but somewhere in a half-glimpsed hinterland on the dirt track to Emmaus, where the Death of God meets the Resurrection, where the supernatural Christ meets the historical Jesus, and where the revolution liberates both the oppressed and the oppressors.

Welcome to Christian Alternative... a space at the edge where the light shines through.